CULTOGRAPHIES

CULTOGRAPHIES is a new list of individual studies devoted to the analysis of cult film. The series provides a comprehensive introduction to those films which have attained the coveted status of a cult classic, focusing on their particular appeal, the ways in which they have been conceived, constructed and received, and their place in the broader popular cultural landscape. For more information, please visit www.cultographies.com

Series editors: Ernest Mathijs (University of British Columbia) and Jamie Sexton (University of Wales, Aberystwyth)

OTHER PUBLISHED TITLES IN THE CULTOGRAPHIES SERIES

THE ROCKY HORROR PICTURE SHOW
Jeffrey Weinstock

THIS IS SPINAL TAP
Ethan de Seife

COMING SOON!

BAD TASTE
Jim Barratt

SUPERSTAR: THE KAREN CARPENTER STORY
Glyn Davies

TOUCH OF EVIL
Rick Schmidlin

THE EVIL DEAD
Kate Egan

BLADE RUNNER
Matt Hills

BRING ME THE HEAD OF ALFREDO GARCIA
Ian Cooper

FRANKENSTEIN
Robert Horton

DONNIE DARKO

Geoff King

WALLFLOWER PRESS
LONDON & NEW YORK

First published in Great Britain in 2007 by
Wallflower Press
6 Market Place, London W1W 8AF
www.wallflowerpress.co.uk

A catalogue record for this book is available from the British Library.

ISBN 978-1-905674-51-0 (pbk)

Book design by Elsa Mathern

Printed and bound in Poland; produced by Polskabook

CONTENTS

                              GRETCHEN
                           You're weird.

                              DONNIE
                              Sorry.

                              GRETCHEN
                    No, that was a compliment.

INTRODUCTION

DONNIE DARKO AND ME

It was dark, brooding and more than a little ambiguous. The ending was something of a puzzler; questions lurked afterwards, along with an uncertainty of mood, a combination of sadness with satisfaction that no easy way out had been taken. It closed with a touching *frisson*, the self-sacrificial death of the hero and a poignant epilogue. It had distinct touches of the 'off-beat', whatever that really means; stylised flourishes, an evocative soundtrack, a general 'atmosphere' greater than the sum of its parts and not immediately easy to pin down. Most of all, though, it was one of those refreshing films, all too rare in commercially-distributed cinema, the direction of which was hard to predict, moment-by-moment, as it progressed. It seemed to mix a number of different qualities, drawing on a range of generic inheritances, thus not simply fitting into the familiar templates associated with any one of them alone.

When I first saw *Donnie Darko*, in the UK in October 2002, it already came with the vague imprint of 'cult' status. It had come onto my radar as a film of interest both personal and professional/academic, the two dimensions far from easy to separate. I was starting a book about American independent cinema, so this was very much the kind of film about which I was thinking at the time.[1] It is also the type to which I am attracted for more general reasons of personal pleasure, the basis of which will be considered further below. I saw the film more or less cold, having gained a general impression that it seemed interesting and had already generated some kind of cult reputation, but without having read any reviews, seen the trailer or followed its earlier commercial progress. As with other films of more than average interest, I wanted to experience it, initially at least, without the intervention of any prior interpretation, beyond those unavoidably gained from elements such as the title, the promotional artwork and a kind of cultural osmosis through which a general sense of its compass was gained in advance (although it is next to impossible, in our culture, especially as someone with a professional interest in American cinema, to see any such film entirely without the acquisition of preconceptions).

Donnie Darko certainly repaid this kind of prior non-investment, something that requires more conscious effort than inadvertently imbibing the trailer or one of the written or broadcast reviews. It is the type of film that is better, first time around, the less you know about it, given the luxury of unfolding at its own pace and without the setting of too many prior expectations. Like many others, I was keen to see it a second time, although in my case this had to await the DVD release some months later. It stood up very well to that second viewing. Some aspects of the story became slightly clearer, but the sense of mystery remained strong and the ending gained increased impact, especially the sequences orchestrated to the strains of 'Mad World'. I came back, again, for the director's cut, although shared with many fans of the film a strong preference for the greater ambiguity of the original.

But why this film as an object of affection or even something bordering for some on mild obsession? I could not claim the latter status myself, having not been initiated into key aspects of the backstory provided on the *Donnie Darko* website or got around to exploring the extras on the original DVD before the release of the director's cut; my initial engagement was somewhat 'lightweight', limited to the film itself, as a more traditionally bounded text. It is the kind of film to which I would gravitate at a personal level, as indicated above, regardless of academic context; a film marked off as distinctive from the productions of mainstream Hollywood, but also accessible. Its departures are sufficient to provide a sense of consuming something different, and thus establishing myself as someone with tastes wider than those of the dominant blockbuster- or star-oriented Hollywood mainstream. It was a film to be seen, by choice, not at either of my local multiplexes, in Brighton, but at the Duke of York's, the city's long-established art, indie and otherwise 'specialist' cinema. It is the kind of film designed, implicitly, to flatter such preferences and orientations, the broader cultural dynamics of which – far from innocent – will be considered elsewhere in this book. But it remains, recognisably, a commercially-oriented version of indie cinema, its distinctiveness marked by relatively small touches within more familiar confines.

Some of the pleasures that *Donnie Darko* offers, and which I was happy to indulge, are those of difference: the reluctance to resolve key narrative issues, the unusual generic blend, the relatively unpredictable direction of the storyline on first viewing. Others are more conventional, including the basic confection of being absorbed in an audio-visually pleasing fictional world, if in this case one that straddles the borders of 'realism' and fantasy. It is far from being a 'difficult' work of modernist art cinema or a production that challenges in any substantial manner at political or social-cultural levels. It is, ultimately, a form of escapist entertainment – creating an alternative, imaginary universe in which life is vivid, heightened and dramatic, in comparison with the world of routine daily life – for particular niche segments of the audience, including myself; those likely to be attracted by its particular mixture of elements from a range of generic and other sources. The pleasures of *Donnie Darko* extend, in my case, into the numerous repeat viewings of the film required for the completion of a study such as this, the process of academic analysis licensing an indulgence that might otherwise be harder to justify. Most if not all of the original pleasure has remained intact each time I have returned to the film, even with pen and paper at hand to make notes on whichever element might have been the principal subject of attention on any particular viewing; which is, perhaps, testament enough.

1

'AN IMPRESSIVE FAILURE': PRODUCTION, PROMOTION AND INITIAL RECEPTION

The story of the production and initial fate of *Donnie Darko* is very much the material of which later cult reputations are often made. The tale of a youth haunted by visions of a rather scary giant rabbit-person was an unlikely-seeming project for a young, first-time filmmaker to get off the ground. The originality of the script was admired by many as it did the rounds within Hollywood, but Richard Kelly's demand to direct, rather than just sell the screenplay as a property or use it as a calling card, was widely viewed as unrealistic. A couple of lucky breaks saw the film into production and its prospects appeared rosy when it opened the 2001 Sundance Film Festival as one of the event's most talked-about titles. Finding a distributor proved difficult, however, and when *Donnie Darko* eventually appeared in cinemas in October 2001 it performed poorly, not helped by the proximity of its release to the events of 9/11. Cult status often requires a sense of a project's embattlement and/or its initial failure to find an audience in this way (which might have been of little comfort to Kelly in the autumn of

2001). The latter is especially important, opening up the space for a title to be 'discovered' by viewers through means other than a standard release and its accompanying promotional and other 'official' discourses such as mainstream reviews.

Many of the textual features of *Donnie Darko* are of a kind that fit the bill for potential cult status, as will be elaborated at greater length below. But cult status implies more than just the characteristics of the film itself. It is a matter of reputation, and thus something that has to be acquired through a particular kind of relationship with viewers. Audience engagement 'remains the acid test of the media cult', as Matt Hills puts it (2002: 136); specific textual qualities can often be identified that create the potential for such engagement, but the latter can never be guaranteed by textual features alone. Cult adoption often includes a negative dimension: a sense of rejection by what is perceived to be the 'general' or 'mainstream' audience, followed by take-up by a particular constituency. In the case of *Donnie Darko*, the initial rejection appeared clear enough. The building of a cult reputation came soon afterwards, however, and through one of the classic routes, established during the 1970s: the 'midnight movie' screening. In one cinema in Manhattan, the film played consecutively for 28 months – by which time, after its DVD release and success overseas, especially in the UK, the cult status of *Donnie Darko* was established to the point at which the film achieved theatrical re-release in a director's cut version, an unprecedented development for an initially unsuccessful production from a first-time writer-director. Another marker of the status it achieved in the wider cinematic landscape was the subsequent use of the title as a point of reference in the marketing of other films that sought to locate themselves in the same kind of arena, examples including *Primer* (2004; '*Donnie Darko* for Grownups') and *Brick* (2005; 'This Year's *Donnie Darko*').[2]

All of which must have seemed a distant prospect back in 1999, when Kelly was seeking studio backing for his project. Here, too, the progress of *Donnie Darko* came in fits and starts, fortunate breaks being followed by a process of frustration familiar to many seeking to break into the industry. Kelly's early good fortune was to be signed up by the powerful Creative Artists Agency (CAA) on the basis of the screenplay. This was a major achievement, given the central role played by the top agencies in the shaping of which projects eventually make it into production. It took the script of *Donnie Darko* to first base, ensuring that it would be read by studio executives, and gave the project some momentum. Kelly spent a year pitching the film, to mixed reactions. Some were genuinely interested in the project, but the dark and ambiguous nature of the screenplay made it hard to convince the studios of its commercial potential, while many refused to take seriously the fresh-faced Kelly's demand that he direct. He was advised to use the script as a writing sample, a demonstration of his credentials, but to focus his efforts on producing something more conventional.[3] At this stage, Kelly was in his mid-twenties, having recently finished film school at the University of Southern California, Los Angeles. He had worked on a couple of scripts to pay the bills, but wanted *Donnie Darko* to be his first feature and thus he persisted. Eventually, he got another break.

The script, by now generally considered to be dead in the water, was read by Jason Schwartzman, star of Wes Anderson's well-received high-school feature *Rushmore* (1998). Schwartzman became attached to the project and, although far from a major name despite being the nephew of Francis Ford Coppola, gave it a new lease of life (although he subsequently pulled out because of other commitments). An offer to produce the film for $2.5 million came from Pandora Films, the 'speciality' label of the non-studio-affiliated Nashville-based Gaylord Entertainment, other interests of which included hotels, television operations, sports management and music publishing. At the same time, Schwartzman's agent sent the script to Flower Films, a production outfit run by the star Drew Barrymore and producer Nancy Juvonen. In another helping of the material of which subsequent cult legends are made, Kelly and his producer Sean McKittrick met Barrymore and Juvonen on the set of *Charlie's Angels* (2000). Kelly asked Barrymore to play the English teacher Karen Pomeroy and Barrymore agreed, if her company could help produce the film. They shook hands, Barrymore became executive producer and the budget, from Pandora, climbed to a more practical $4.5 million (Scott 2003: xxxv). It was at this point that *Donnie Darko* became a reality, largely on the back of traditional Hollywood star power, with Barrymore in a role defined by Kelly as that of 'mentor and godmother' (Scott 2003: xxxvi). The presence of Barrymore helped attract other performers to the project, eventually including Jake Gyllenhaal instead of Schwartzman in the central role as Donnie and a strong team of supporting players including Mary McDonnell, Patrick Swayze, Katherine Ross, Noah Wyle and Holmes Osborne.

Barrymore contributed in more ways than one to the (eventual) success of *Donnie Darko*. Her name gave the project more weight, while she also agreed to work for the basic union 'scale' wages, setting a precedent for others involved in the production. Another who agreed to cut his rate was the director of photography, Steven Poster, a name that stood out to Kelly from a number of others considered by himself and McKittrick on the basis of his previous collaboration with Ridley Scott on *Someone to Watch Over Me* (1987). Poster and his regular crew brought with them what Kelly describes as many 'luxuries', including access to anamorphic lenses, usually too costly to be considered on low-budget productions, and other equipment obtained in a cut-rate deal through the cinematographer's existing relationship with the camera-equipment provider Panavision. It is to Poster that Kelly credits the look of the film, a visual quality that belies the low budget (Scott 2003: xxxvi–viii).

Donnie Darko was shot in 28 days – a nice cultish touch, the same period as that given to Donnie as the deadline after which the world will end. It was a tight schedule, described by Kelly as 'relentless' (Scott 2003: xlviii), although the film came in on time as a result of what Poster describes as a combination of careful planning and on-the-spot improvisation.[4] Simultaneous shooting of separate elements was used to speed up the process in some cases. While one camera was shooting Donnie at the microphone in a sequence in which he responds to a presentation by the lifestyle guru Jim Cunningham (Patrick Swayze), for example, a second was getting reaction shots from other members of the audience. While a real school stood in for one of the key locations, the fictional Middlesex Ridge School, parts of the premises were dressed as other sets to enable additional scenes to be squeezed into the same days of shooting. For the climactic scenes outside the house of the elderly Roberta Sparrow (Patience Cleveland) some 35 camera set-ups were required during the darkness of a short night in August. In this and some other instances, including the Cunningham seminar, economy and logistics dictated the use of hand-held camerawork, although this also provided an appropriately edgy quality to the images that resulted. As a general rule, shooting was kept tight, and only a minimal amount of 'coverage' – extra insurance footage to guard against unforeseen problems of performance or continuity – was produced. The editing process that followed was clearly contentious. Debates about the length of the film and what should or should not be cut became 'very confrontational and upsetting' on some occasions, Kelly suggests,

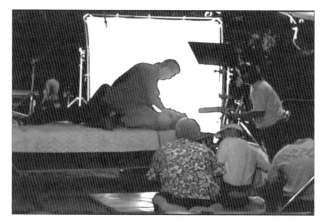

One of the 35 set-ups achieved during a single night's shooting outside the house of Roberta Sparrow

although his claim to have 'won almost every battle' seems belied by his DVD commentary on a number of scenes deleted from the original that he had been keen to include (Scott 2003: xlvi).

And so, eventually, *Donnie Darko* headed for Sundance, and what was to prove a mixture of fortunes typical of the life cycle of the film. It went into the festival with a status that cannot easily be bought (even with the services of a good publicist): the amorphous sense of expectations and currency known in the trade as 'buzz', a notoriously slippery quality that can as easily backfire as be converted into concrete benefits such as an attractive deal with a distributor. For *Donnie Darko*, the buzz turned rapidly from positive to negative. The festival began with a Friday night screening, packed with representatives from the leading independent distributors. Harvey Weinstein, then head of Miramax, the Disney-owned subsidiary and dominant player in the sector, emerged from the screening wearing a *Donnie Darko* baseball cap. Miramax executives were described as huddling 'intensely' outside the theatre (Mohr 2001a), creating expectations of the kind of deal for which Miramax was notorious: a pre-emptive strike in which big money is talked in exchange for an early and exclusive commitment from the filmmakers. But nothing happened. Exactly why is unclear, but it seems likely that the film suffered from a form of game-playing that often surrounds the embattled process of indie acquisitions. According to one report, Miramax made an offer but withdrew it in the face of negative reaction to the film from other distributors (Mohr 2001b). A similar process is described by Kelly, who suggests that many distributors talked the film down at the end of the screening in order to discourage competition from other potential buyers (Scott 2003: xlvii). Whatever the exact case, the outcome was that *Donnie Darko* left Sundance without a distribution deal, a position that appeared all the worse, in terms of the film's future prospects, given the initially high expectations. One unnamed 'top indie exec' was quoted describing it as an 'impressive failure', useful currency in the acquisition of cult status (exactly the kind of 'official' verdict that suggests a film might lend itself to cult adoption) but of little help in the achievement of initial distribution.[5]

The bottom line at Sundance, as elsewhere, seemed to be that *Donnie Darko* was hard to categorise, another cult-worthy credential but one that made industry figures tread warily. In Sundance-specific terms, the film fitted the bill in several respects. Kelly was listed by *Variety* as one of 'a new breed of auteur' who emerged at the festival, figures with 'an unyielding determination' to direct their own scripts and the authority 'to elicit strong performances from gifted casts' (Chagollan 2001). The film's combination of more and less marketable elements pitched it about right for Sundance, and the commercial end of the indie spectrum more generally; enough to mark it out as distinctive from the mainstream, but with sufficient hooks to help it find a substantial niche. But, with that, also came criticism from those who saw themselves as defenders of the independent faith. *Donnie Darko* was cited in some circles as emblematic of a trend away from more 'personal' material and towards products reliant on genre – not to mention (the term 'gasp' was used in one trade industry feature) its use of special effects, an issue debated at one seminar forum during the festival (Williams 2001).

Post-Sundance, prospects for *Donnie Darko* seemed almost as grim as those faced by its protagonist. After continuing to languish without a distributor, it came close to being released directly to cable television, a fate generally regarded as equal to death as far as the cinematic career of the filmmaker is concerned (and, arguably, a more difficult route back even for cult reappropriation). But *Donnie Darko* was to get another saviour, in the shape of Newmarket Films, a former finance company that had turned distributor to come to the rescue of Christopher Nolan's *Memento* (2000). *Memento*, like *Donnie Darko*, took an unconventional approach to generically-based material (in this case, a revenge thriller told mostly backwards) that struggled to find a distributor. It was eventually handled by the former exhibitor Bob Berney, funded by the film's production company, Newmarket Capital Group. Berney was also involved in the distribution of *Donnie Darko*, for which Newmarket negotiated a 'service deal' for distribution by IFC Films (the distribution arm of the Independent Film Channel, to which Berney had subsequently moved). In a service deal, the distributor is paid to provide a theatrical release when a more conventional deal is not forthcoming, a practice that became increasingly common in some cases in the early 2000s (rather than, as usual, the distributor having to pay for the privilege, along with putting up funds for costs such as prints and advertising). At the time of Newmarket's approach, Kelly reports, he begged his financiers to accept the deal, which they did – even though more immediate money was on offer from a cable company – to avoid the opprobrium associated with a low-status direct-to-cable or video release. At the time that the deal was announced, *Memento* was relatively early in its release but already performing more than healthily, having taken some $8.5 million of an eventual $25 million US gross.[6] It turned out, against expectations, to be the indie hit of the year. A similar performance might have been anticipated for *Donnie Darko*, but that was not to be the case.

Donnie Darko was slated for a Halloween-week release, perfect timing for a dark work, sold to a large extent as a horror film, in which Halloween itself featured prominently during the latter stages of the narrative. Autumn is also a slot often favoured for independent features, avoiding the intense blockbuster-scale competition typical of the summer and Christmas holiday months and strategically positioned during the build-up to the major awards season. But this autumn was to be different from any other in recent US history, marked by the attacks that included the destruction of the twin towers of the World Trade Center. The events of 9/11 appear to have impacted on the fate of the film on several levels. In more general terms, they were widely considered to have done little to increase the appetite of filmgoers for dark and disturbing material, particularly in an immediate post-9/11 period marked by anthrax and other 'terrorist'-related scares. Of more specific concern was the fact that a prominent part of the plot revolved around the destruction caused by a jet engine falling from the sky, in uncomfortable if only partial resonance with the recent events. If that was not enough, another jet crashed in the New York borough of Queens two weeks after the opening of the film, initial speculation about the cause (eventually proved wrong) including suggestions that an engine had fallen from the plane. The fall-out from 9/11 also had a more immediate effect in disrupting

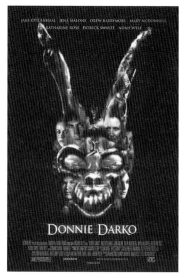

The main poster artwork

the film's publicity campaign, much of which was lost in the weeks leading up to the release weekend (Scott 2003: xlix). No changes were made to the film, but shots involving the jet engine were pulled from the trailer in response to potential audience sensitivity (Hundley 2001).

From the title onwards, *Donnie Darko* was sold as a film with dark, troubling dimensions, although the diminutive 'Donnie' has a certain lightening effect. The title also has comic book resonances, in keeping with Donnie's destiny to become a kind of super-hero. The principal artwork used on the main poster and the initial video/DVD release establishes a clear association with horror, reinforced by the choice of a Halloween opening. A disturbing, skull-like mask, what will prove to be the Halloween-mask visage of Frank (James Duval), is overlaid with, and partially comprised of, the faces of

14

cast members. The image, in a cool, steely blue, is set against a plain black background. At the top of the poster, in modest capitals, is a list of cast names, suggesting an ensemble rather than star-led emphasis, and leaving the horror-genre component to dominate the foreground. The film title, at the bottom, is in a typeface with modern gothic associations, contributing to the emphasis on horror, the white lettering given a dynamic blur-shading effect that adds a further impression of otherworldliness. The overall effect is quite clear-cut and one-dimensional, although the concerned expressions of the faces, when examined more closely, perhaps suggest a greater focus on character relationship than might typically be associated with mainstream horror.

Trailers for the film, not being restricted to the one-shot approach of the poster, have the space to articulate a more subtle blend of resonances. The primary note remains 'troubling', 'dark' and potentially disturbing, but less unambiguously located within a horror context. The full-length theatrical trailer establishes a mixture of associations, starting with an emphasis on the experiences of a 'troubled teenager' but quickly blending this with intimations of the presence of otherworldly forces and dimensions, including an element of science fiction in explicit references to time travel. The generic resonances are thus made more complex. The dimension of the film that can be associated more widely with teen coming-of-age drama is given substantial space. The otherworldly remains dominant, however, as the trailer develops, partly because explicit references to quotidian subject matter such as 'the pain of puberty' (an extract taken from a reading of Graham Greene's 'The Destructors' (1954)) are verbal, from a number of characters, and tend to be countered by fragmentary images that appear to realise the supra-normal (Frank in the rabbit suit, a 'portal' opening on a cinema screen, 'unnatural' cloud formations above Donnie's house, and a frequent use of stylised and/or accelerated-motion imagery that in itself seems to manifest something beyond the fabric of the everyday). We hear a character quite clearly identified as Donnie's therapist (Katherine Ross) refer to 'daylight hallucinations', which the images might be taken to be, but at other levels the discourse of the trailer suggests differently. Titles, shown alone on the screen and interspersed between images from the film, provide what seems to be a more authoritative, because non-diegetically located, source of commentary (clearly imposed externally on the material rather than being caught up in tensions between the real and imaginary that the trailer elsewhere signals as a part of the diegetic fabric). The first series of these is 'visions', 'time travel' and 'sacrifice', associated both with imagery that seems to give them substance and with the trailer's overall development in a direction in which such dimensions appear to be taken increasingly seriously. A second pair adds to this impression by stating 'the only way to unwind the future … is to follow the path'. A third series, based more on establishing mood, gives us 'Dark', 'Darkest', 'Darko', amid sequences cut increasingly fast and building towards a crescendo of sound and imagery. Throughout, the trailer is accompanied by music and other sound effects that play a central role in the creation of an overall mood of darkness and dread, particularly a repetitive and throbbing bass theme that suggests an unrelenting drive towards some dark encounter with destiny (the 'Manipulated Living' theme from the score by Michael Andrews).

Five shorter television spot adverts were produced, drawing primarily on the same set of fragments mobilised in the theatrical version.[7] These are generally faster moving and 'thinner' in texture than the cinema trailer and demonstrate several different points of emphasis within the same broad equation. Two draw explicitly on the Halloween (and therefore horror) connection, one in an on-screen title, another in the voice-over (and all of the TV spots use the clichéd impossibly-gravel-voiced movie trailer intonation noticeable for its absence from the theatrical version). One organises its other sound and images around the 'visions', 'time travel', 'sacrifice' strand of titles; two, slightly altered from the theatrical, around 'Dark', 'Darker' (rather than 'Darkest') and 'Darko'. In one case, a voice-over imposes a more conventional and containing romantic framework on the material. 'A young man has come to the end of an era', it declares. 'Now, the only way to save what he loves … [image of Donnie kissing Gretchen (Jena Malone)] is to follow what he fears.' Whatever 'dark' subject matter is evoked, the dynamic is reduced here, at least partially, to a more domestic agenda. Another spot puts its emphasis almost entirely on the cast, following its opening-voiced 'this Halloween' by listing all the names of the principals. This might also be understood as creating relative distance from the darker elements of the material, a focus on players rather than narrative substance, although the performers are generally depicted with troubled expressions that convey a sense of the overall tone.

The mixed resonances suggested by the full-length trailer were certainly picked up by major American critics when the film was released on 28 October 2001. Whether the blend of generic and other ingredients was seen as a strength or a weakness was a matter of dispute. For the *Los Angeles Times* reviewer, *Donnie Darko*, 'like its defiant hero … rebels against simplistic classifications' and effects 'with stunning self-confidence a risky shift in tone from the citrus-y domestic banter of its opening 15 minutes to the Stephen King-like chills of its Halloween-set denouement' (Stuart 2001). J. Hoberman (2001), in the niche-market New York *Village Voice*, declared it 'certainly the most original and venturesome indie I've seen this year', while the large circulation *New York Post* agreed that it was 'the year's most ambiguous indie, a sprawling comic sci-fi fantasy that's an awfully impressive writing-directing debut', even if one with 'third-act problems' (Lumenick 2001). Reviewers who gave mixed responses often did so on the basis of what were seen as the uncertain tone and direction of the film. For the *San Francisco Chronicle* 'It starts out as a suburban satire … turns into a psychological drama with an amazing twist [then] takes a wild leap into the unknown with a sci-fi foray into "worm holes" in the universe, and time travel'; the reviewer's conclusion: 'If this movie ever figured out what it wanted to be when it grows up, it would be a terrific one' (Graham 2001). For Roger Ebert (2001), in the *Chicago Sun-Times*, the 'set up and development is fascinating, the payoff less so', Kelly being accused of losing control in the final scenes. *The New York Times* describes *Donnie Darko* as 'a wobbly cannonball of a movie' with shifts of mood Kelly does not have the assurance to pull off: 'He labours to bring science fiction, grim comedy and social satire into his story of a haunted misfit.' The loyalty of the cast to the director's vision is evident, the reviewer concludes; 'the director just hasn't figured out what that vision is' (Mitchell 2001).

The reviews further demonstrate two of the dominant pulls exerted by the film. On the one hand, it had from the start potential to be taken up strongly in some circles, and to generate cult appeal, partly because it was difficult to categorise (although also because of the specific generic territories it crossed, as will be suggested below). On the other, some of the same factors gave it a potential frailty at the box office if localised appeal failed to crystallise beyond a narrow constituency. For admirers such as J. Hoberman and Jan Stuart, in the *Los Angeles Times*, the 9/11 connection only added to its resonance. On second viewing in this context for Stuart (2001), who first encountered *Donnie Darko* at Sundance 'and took in its hybrid of styles with decided scepticism', the film's 'transforming accident and its yearning to turn back the clock on tragic events takes on a potency and relevancy that are almost unbearably moving'. For Hoberman (2001), similarly, contemporary events rendered the film 'weirdly consoling'. Although a period piece, it 'seems perfectly attuned to the present moment'; 'a splendid debut under any circumstances ... released for Halloween 2001, it has uncanny gravitas'.

Cinema audiences did not seem to agree. Or, if they did, it did not seem to be what they were looking for at the time. *Donnie Darko* bombed on release. It opened in the US on 58 screens in eight cities: more than the smallest of 'platform' releases, in which 'specialist' films are opened in only a couple of cities before seeking to build gradually through review coverage and word-of-mouth, but still a small scale, in keeping with the usual strategy for indie features (as opposed to the release of contemporary blockbusters on up to 7,000 separate screens to the accompaniment of nationwide television advertising). It took a dismal $110,494 on its opening weekend and was withdrawn from more than half its screens in the following week, the second weekend gross dropping to $58,435.[8] By the end of its run, the total was a meagre $514,545, a distinct failure. Kelly blames the poor performance on the distribution strategy, arguing that the film was opened too wide. It played very well in New York and Los Angeles, he suggests, the two cities usually targeted in narrower platform releases, 'but the theatres were empty in Washington, DC, Chicago and Seattle' (Scott 2003: xlix).[9] As a result, the overall opening figures looked bad and investment in the film was reduced, as is common practice in Hollywood and, increasingly, the independent sector. The newspaper adverts and other forms of marketing were pulled, Kelly says, leaving the film to die out slowly, when it might have been more successful had it been left to build through its stronger venues in New York and Los Angeles. Not that Kelly gives the impression of being particularly embittered about what happened; his film did, at least, get a theatrical release. And, left to its own devices on a shrinking number of screens (down to single figures by the end of November), it did not simply wither on the vine; its cult status began to ripen.

2

AFTERLIFE

Its initial release having fizzled out, for whatever reason, *Donnie Darko* began to build a following through the 'back channels' of popular culture; sites populated by those whose enthusiasm and engagement helped to sustain ongoing word-of-mouth appreciation of the film, fuelling it for a return to a larger audience. It benefited from a combination of more and less recently established routes into the world of cult recognition. First was its life on the 'midnight movie' circuit, initially at the Pioneer Theater in Manhattan's East Village, where *Donnie Darko* played continuously until the release of the director's cut in July 2004. Here, the film gained association with another source of cult status, related in this case to a particular kind of viewing context. The 'midnight movie', a forum established in the 1970s through screenings of titles such as *Pink Flamingos* (1970), *The Rocky Horror Picture Show* (1975) and *Eraserhead* (1978), implies a transgression of the usual boundaries of filmgoing. As J. P. Telotte suggests: 'We go to see these films not just after dark but at a kind of magical time: the "witching hour", the point when one day becomes another' (1991b: 103). Telotte suggests that such screenings also imply a 'magical' change in the status of the venue, even in the most conventional multiplex, the theatre shifting in character 'from a model of industrialised and efficient exhibition practices to a kind of "underground" cinema, an urban (or suburban) site of ritualistic activity' (ibid.). The midnight movie connotes a sense of special occasion, when most filmgoers are safely tucked up in their beds, that marks out both film and viewer from normal routines of exhibition/consumption, even if it retains its own commercial logic for the exhibitors concerned (on the latter, see Jancovich 2002).

Dimensions of cult such as viewing conditions and textual features are often closely interconnected, particular qualities in the film usually lending themselves in one way or another to treatments such as midnight screenings. Another dimension of *Donnie Darko* central to its achievement of cult status, and to its specific ability to prosper through secondary channels of discourse, beyond the text itself, is its explicit openness to a range of interpretations. This is true at the levels of both basic comprehension of certain key narrative events – what exactly 'happens', in some cases, or what is the status of the material – and broader interpretations, once a particular version of narrative events is established. All texts are open to a variety of potential interpretations, however much they might seek to encourage particular readings. Textual material alone does not guarantee the fixing of any interpretive outcome. A number of other factors can come into play, most obviously the potentially variable frames of reference brought by viewers from different socio-cultural backgrounds. Most cinematic and other texts are designed in such a way as to encourage particular 'preferred' readings, however. This is true of *Donnie Darko* in many respects, but the film also includes areas of ambiguity that invite the viewer to play a more overtly and consciously active role than usual in the process of narrative resolution, an issue addressed in more detail in chapter three.[10] It is here in particular that the film lends itself to being sustained through more recently established media such as internet sites and DVD commentary and extras: potentially cult reputation-building channels of the digital age that played an important role in the renaissance of *Donnie Darko*.

In its original incarnation, *Donnie Darko* leaves plenty of questions unanswered and many issues at best partly resolved. Is the time travel dimension apparently uncovered by Donnie 'real', for example, or can many of the events of the film be attributed to his disturbed state of mind? Exactly how coherent is the climax of the film, if we go along with the former interpretation: to what extent can everything else be fitted into its logic? Such issues were a source of complaint for some critics. But the questions invited by the film are also a major source of its potential appeal, and especially its longevity as a part of the landscape of popular (sub)culture. A major qualification for some texts that generate 'fan' activity, as John Fiske suggests, is that they are 'producerly', by which he means texts that generate more than usual amounts of interpretive and other activity by their followers; 'they have to be open, to contain gaps, irresolutions, contradictions, which both allow and invite fan productivity' (1992: 42). While this might not be essential in every case, the same quality is emphasised in a number of other accounts of fan activity and/or definitions of cult status; the 'perpetual hermeneutic' of John Tulloch and Manuel Alvarado (1983: 133) or the 'endlessly deferred narrative' of Matt Hills (2002: 143). Hills makes a useful distinction between how this tends to work in cult texts such as *Donnie Darko* and unresolved formats such as television soap opera, the latter having multiple ongoing narrative strands: 'The cult form, by contrast, typically focuses its endlessly deferred narrative around a singular question or related set of questions' (2002: 134).[11] *Donnie Darko* is a good example of a text that lends itself to this process, particularly at the level of interpretive activity generated from a range of official and unofficial sources that maintained the currency of the film after its initial release.

Donnie Darko began from a position of intentional ambiguity, according to Kelly. 'When I started writing the script', he says, 'I was so afraid that if I clarified the ending any more than I did, the film would collapse under its own pretension' (in Scott 2003: xxv). During the period in which it was being readied for release, however, he wrote several pages that would be presented as extracts from 'The Philosophy of Time Travel', the imaginary book written by Roberta Sparrow. It was an attempt to explain key aspects of the film but to do so outside the text, according to this account, without robbing the film itself of its central enigmas. 'The Philosophy of Time Travel' offered just one theory, Kelly suggests, not meant to be definitive. It was written from the perspective of another viewer of the film rather than that of its maker, he says, although such a disclaimer became hard to sustain as his explanation moved from a position of marginality to one increasingly closer to the heart of the film (Scott 2003: xxxii). Kelly gives a slightly different account in his commentary on the director's cut DVD, where he says the extracts were written during the editing process and any thought of including them within the film had to be abandoned when the rough cut came in at two-and-a-half hours and already required excisions. The implication here is that he had considered working them into the original version. Either way, the creation of this background explanation proved to be a canny move on Kelly's part, creating a focal point for interpretative speculation about the film and providing a significant and marketable 'extra' for the DVD release and subsequent director's cut. Its first outing, however, was on the official website for the film, which also supplied a number of other sources of backstory and information. The website takes the form of a puzzle structure rather than providing standard ingredients such as plot summary, clips, stills and production notes. The visitor is invited to work through three 'levels', like those of a simple computer game, providing answers to a series of questions in order to proceed. Backstory information includes psychiatric reports on Donnie from a period before that covered by the film, 'newspaper' archive reports relating to other characters including Kenneth Monnitoff (Noah Wyle) and Cunningham, the findings of tests carried out on the jet engine that falls on the Darko house and Kelly's pages from 'The Philosophy of Time Travel'. The latter set out the key points of an interpretation according to which Donnie is recruited as a 'Living Receiver' to prevent an apocalypse resulting from a rift in the fabric of space-time (the manifestation of which is a jet engine falling into his world from the future), an event that creates an unstable 'Tangent Universe' that threatens the existence of the 'Primary Universe'.

Plenty of others soon followed Kelly into online discussions and interpretations.[12] As the writer-director himself suggests, his explanation probably increased rather than diminished the number of questions left unanswered, further sustaining debate and interest in the film (Scott 2003: xxxii). Web-based discussion and the geographically very limited availability of *Donnie Darko* in cinemas (midnight screenings or otherwise) can be assumed to have played a considerable role in the creation of demand for the video/DVD release, which proved highly successful. Domestic sales of the DVD amounted to more than $10 million after the launch in March 2002, some twenty times the original theatrical gross and a huge boost to the industrial standing of the film (not to mention Kelly's future prospects) (see Burnett 2004; Snyder 2004). With the DVD came the obligatory 'extras', added-value components that contributed to debates about the film. These included 'The Philosophy of Time Travel', a number of deleted scenes, trailers, original artwork by Kelly and – the main original contribution of the DVD – an audio commentary by Kelly and Jake Gyllenhaal. In the hierarchy of interpretations, commentary by the director (especially when a writer-director, and clearly unrivalled 'author' of the film) ranks highest, making this a much-anticipated and highly marketable feature for those with investment in questions of interpretation.

What Kelly offers in the commentary, along with numerous asides and interruptions from Gyllenhaal, is very much in keeping with the interpretation grounded in 'The Philosophy of Time Travel'. 'Right here we are entering into a parallel universe, a Tangent Universe', he explains, as the camera shows the clock reading midnight, some eight minutes into the film. Clear guidance is offered to the viewer on how to interpret key aspects of the narrative. When Gyllenhaal raises the issue of the sanity or insanity of Donnie, Kelly is quick to respond: 'For me there is no insanity. This is a science fiction story for me and Donnie is hyper-aware, he's hyper-sensitive, and he's been chosen to perform a task.' Donnie is, indeed, a super-hero, Kelly suggests, pointing out as the film progresses how each of the secondary characters plays a part in guiding him towards his destiny: 'There's a point to everything; it's all there for a reason.' Seemingly arbitrary or relatively minor events turn out to be highly motivated, all working towards a particular agenda. This interpretation, as manifested in the DVD commentary, occupies a liminal position, on the margins of the text. It is not integrated into the primary text, the film itself, in which any such reading is far from readily apparent. Kelly's reading requires a particular kind of viewing in order to be mobilised (or prior engagement via web materials), and a viewer sufficiently motivated to re-watch the film with the commentary replacing most of the original sound, an experience created by the capabilities of DVD and likely to appeal to far from all potential viewers of the film.

Having achieved a commercially-respectable variety of cult status via midnight movie screenings, internet debate and its rebound on DVD, *Donnie Darko* gained a head of steam that helped it to greater theatrical success overseas – especially in the UK – than it had enjoyed in the US. The opening week-end performance, just before Halloween 2002, out-grossed its US equivalent (£191,348) on fewer screens (37). The film went on to gross a UK total equivalent to $2.5 million, several times the total taken in the US, a rare disparity for an American feature given the vastly larger size of the US market. Its greater success in the UK has partly been attributed to the use of marketing strategies that sought to create unconventional sources of advance awareness of the film, including the distribution in London of hand-coloured stickers and posters featuring the title and the rabbit mask along with promotional artwork created after the film was shown to a group of leading graffiti artists.[13] Press reviews were generally positive or mixed-to-positive, with some exceptions. For the mid-

Teaser artwork used ahead of the UK release

market *Daily Mail* the film was 'a shambles'; 'part sci-fi, part psychological thriller, all pretentious mess', but appreciative reviews were found across the spectrum, from the liberal end of the *Guardian* and the *Observer* to the conservative *Daily Telegraph* and mass-market *Sun*.[14] *Donnie Darko* may also have gained, at this point and in subsequent DVD incarnations, from a contemporary vogue for 1980s British bands such as Echo and the Bunnymen and Tears for Fears, which feature prominently on the soundtrack.[15] The UK video/DVD release in May 2003 resulted in sales of more than 150,000 copies within four months, single-handedly boosting the fortunes of the distributor Metrodome and its German parent TV Loonland (Roxborough 2003). The final touch was the surprise achievement of a Christmas 2003 number one in the UK singles chart by Gary Jules' version of the song 'Mad World', which features prominently in the closing scenes of the film, a move by one component of the film into a mainstream popular culture realm very different from that usually associated with the status of cult (the Christmas number one slot having a reputation, from many past exemplars, as a touchstone for unchallenging schmaltz).

It was at about this time, late 2003, that Kelly and Bob Berney, the distributor, attended a screening that marked the film's first anniversary at the Pioneer. Berney raised the possibility of a theatrical re-release, starting a discussion that culminated in the release of the director's cut the following June (Burnett 2004). The creation of the director's cut marked the point at which explanatory material that had existed at the margins – from website and wider internet discussion to DVD extras – moved into the text itself, most notably Kelly's pages from 'The Philosophy of Time Travel'. The result was a significant shift in the nature of the film. Much that remained implicit in the original, and sometimes deeply implicit and hard to explain without outside aid, was made clear and explicit in

'The Philosophy of Time Travel' as a DVD extra

the director's cut. What Kelly provided as an optional extra via the website and then his commentary became central to the fabric of the film, removing much of its ambiguity and offering a more straightforward narrative experience. Extracts from 'The Philosophy of Time Travel' are presented, full-screen, at a number of strategic moments after Dr Monnitoff lends Donnie his copy of the book. Their deployment in this manner makes them increasingly influential in steering the viewer's likely reading of the film, as they are both integrated into the narrative and positioned at particular moments when they serve to clarify the recent, current or forthcoming state of affairs. Particular sections of each extract are highlighted in most cases through visual effects that bring them to the fore, increasing the extent to which the written text is brought to bear in specific detail, rather than as a more general accompaniment to the film.

The result is that the viewer is sometimes led by the nose, at the level of close textual detail. The extract from Chapter 4, 'The Artifact and the Living', for example, provides crucial

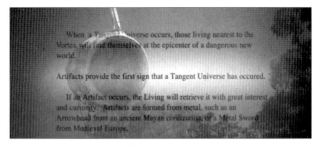

Superimposed narrative guidance: text from 'The Philosophy of Time Travel' spells out the 'artifact' status of the jet engine that crashed on the Darko house

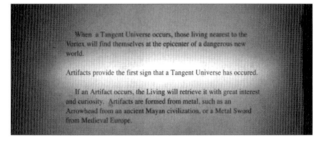

As the image of the jet fades, the relevant part of the text is highlighted

background on the creation of the Tangent Universe. Behind the initial text, superimposed images appear of the aftermath of the jet engine crash on the Darko house, as seen earlier in the film. These dissolve into the image of the engine itself, as it is lifted across the sky by a crane. The engine is singled out briefly, the sole object in the frame, before the image fades and the text moves in towards the screen to highlight a separate central line reading: 'Artifacts provide the first sign that a Tangent Universe has occurred.' That the engine is such an artifact is spelled out explicitly, through cinematic devices almost as clear-cut as the words of any external commentary by the filmmaker. Other such inserts explain both prominent and more subtle dimensions of the film. From Chapter 6, 'The Living Receiver', for example, we are given an explanation for some of Donnie's powers, including 'strength, telekinesis, mind control, and the ability to conjure fire and water'. This helps, post-hoc, to account for his seemingly impossible feat of embedding an axe in the head of a bronze statue after causing a flood at his school, and creates a broad and unspecified rationale for whatever mechanism Donnie uses to achieve the final mending of the rift in space-time around which the plot revolves. It also draws attention to much finer and less overt detail. Immediately after the presentation of this part of 'The Philosophy of Time Travel' comes a sequence in which Donnie finds Jim Cunningham's wallet on the sidewalk outside the latter's mansion. In the background, sprinklers are watering the capacious lawns. Donnie turns and realises the house is Cunningham's. 'Now you know where he lives', comes the disembodied voice of Frank, at which point the sprinklers stop and Donnie looks around as if to identify the cause. In the light of the preceding text, with its phrase 'the ability to conjure fire and water', the stopping of the sprinklers becomes more noticeable and significant, as further evidence of Donnie's powers (earlier, he caused a flood; later he will set fire to Cunningham's house, setting

'Now you know where he lives': Donnie outside Jim Cunningham's house

in train another necessary step in the path of his mission). Without the steer provided by the written text, the viewer has to do much more work if the moment-by-moment connection is to be made.

Another strong intervention from the book comes in what is presented as part of Chapter 9, 'The Ensurance Trap', which reads: 'The Manipulated Dead [those who die during the period of the Tangent Universe and are used as tools in the process of restoration] will set an Ensurance Trap. The Living Receiver must ensure the fate of all mankind.' This is provided during the Halloween party scenes which precede a sequence at the house of Roberta Sparrow that ends in the accidental death of Gretchen and is, again, a major source of narrative clarification. It spells out, effectively, the fact that Gretchen's death has been contrived, as a trap to ensure Donnie's actions: it gives him the personal motivation of being able to reverse her death as one specific outcome of the wider task of repairing the fabric of space-time. This is another central narrative component that is far from entirely clear on initial (and perhaps also subsequent) viewing of the original without outside help. A further example relating to more nuanced effects comes in the final extract, from Chapter 12, 'Dreams', which suggests that when the Manipulated awaken from their journey into the Tangent Universe 'they are often haunted by the experience in their dreams'. This is inserted before the 'Mad World' sequence that begins with Dr Monnitoff awakening from sleep with a puzzled look, followed by images of other characters including a tearful Cunningham, Kitty Farmer (Beth Grant) and Frank, the latter surrounded by evidence of (Primary Universe) designs for his Halloween rabbit costume and raising a hand, questioningly, to the eye in which he is shot towards the climax of the events in the Tangent Universe. Resonances of Manipulated existence remain, in such small touches, including the hesitant exchange of waves between a Gretchen who

Intimations of another existence: Gretchen's tentative wave to Rose after the reversal of previous events

never gets to meet Donnie and his now-bereaved mother as the film draws to a close. The subtlety and originally elusive nature of these effects is altered significantly by the spelling out of their basis in the fantastic reality detailed so explicitly in the director's cut. Space to interpret the events of the film as the outcome of Donnie's state of mind is also constrained by elements added to this version. Dr Thurman (Katherine Ross) reveals that she has been prescribing placebos, rather than real medication, suggesting that she does not believe his problems to be the result of mental incapacity (a very different impression from that given in the scene where she meets his parents and recommends upping his dose). Shortly before this, a sequence is inserted in which Donnie himself declares to his mother, in what will prove to be a final parting, 'there's nothing broken in my brain'.

Many of the new ingredients of the director's cut came from elements included as extras (especially deleted and extended scenes and the pages from 'The Philosophy of Time Travel') on the DVD release of the original. A budget of $290,000 was provided for the new version, some twenty minutes longer, much of it spent on additions to the special effects sequences in which various aspects of the time travel dimension of the film are manifested, along with a richer and improved overall sound quality. Some of the music was also changed, including the early use of the 1980s period track 'Never Tear Us Apart' by INXS, the rights for which had proved too expensive for the original (Burnett 2004). Most of the deleted scenes supplied as extras with the original are included, in whole or in part, a number of which Kelly had described as important to the film and only omitted because he was under pressure to cut the film down to less than two hours. Several of these underpin the explanation of the narrative provided in 'The Philosophy of Time Travel', including the hints given by elements of parallel stories: fragments of a poem read by Donnie (reference to delivery from a coming 'storm', delivery of the children and sending the 'monsters' back underground where no-one can see them, except him) and *Watership Down*, the text replaced in the school's English class after the banning of 'The Destructors' (including another apocalyptic vision). A number of restored scenes also briefly but significantly extend the roles of minor characters, the most important, for Kelly in his commentary, being the 'fatherly advice' sequence in which Eddie Darko (Holmes Osborne) signals a connection with his son and tells him to be honest, whatever happens to him (another of the many sources of guidance in the following of his quest). Some originally deleted scenes that help to spell out the nature of the film's events were withheld from the director's cut, however, most notably an extended version of Donnie's first encounter with Frank ('conversation with Frank') which offers early and explicit hints that what is involved is a form of divine intervention. Another deleted scene not included ('the end is here'), provided among the standard extras with the director's cut edition and accessible as a hidden 'Easter egg' feature on the original, shows Donnie bleeding and twitching in his death throes, impaled on a piece of wreckage after the jet engine falls into his bedroom.[16]

The release of the director's cut was handled differently from that of the original, in apparent vindication of Kelly's criticisms. It premiered at the relatively low-profile Seattle Film Festival in May 2004. Seattle was then used as a test market for six weeks to see how the film performed, before it was taken any wider. It was judged to have done respectably, in suburban areas as well as its more natural home in the urban art-house (Burnett 2004). The new version opened on six screens in New York and Los Angeles on 25 July, grossing $53,000 over the weekend at a much better per-screen average than the original opening in 2001. It was very gradually widened, but only slightly, to a maximum of 22 screens that September, eventually grossing a modest $727,000. The theatrical performance of the director's cut was less than sensational, in other words, but it was a no-lose situation for the distributor, as the trade press suggested at the time. At the very least, the release of a new edition, at no great cost, would give a boost to the existing midnight trade and to the film's cult status and provide the basis for a more profitable new DVD edition.

A new trailer was produced for the director's cut, in which the cult dimension of the film was used explicitly as a marketing hook. 'Newmarket Films Proudly Presents', announces the first title, 'The never before seen director's cut of the cult phenomenon.' 'So ahead of its time you'll have to go back', it continues, 'to believe your eyes.' A connection is made in the phrase 'you'll have to go back' between the time travel dimension of the film and the prescription that it needs to be seen a second time to be understood, a device used on other occasions in the marketing of features with complex or ambiguous narratives (previous such examples include David Lynch's *Mulholland Dr.* (2001)). The overall tone of the new trailer contrasts with that of the original. Visually, it consists primarily of a very fast-cut array of images from the film, opening with a stylised eyeball close-up that foregrounds one of the most noticeable additional visual features of the director's cut. The image sequence is played to music from the 1980s songs on the soundtrack, principally Echo and the Bunnymen's 'Killing Moon' (although, ironically, the track plays a smaller role in the director's cut than it did in the original release). The music, especially, creates a less dark and gloomy overall resonance than that of the original trailer, as does rapid-fire editing that does not dwell on any particular sequence or provide space for any dialogue. The trailer ends, as it starts, on a self-congratulatory note, the final titles 'Are you ready?' and 'Coming this summer' being accompanied by background applause taken from the reaction to the Sparkle Motion school dance troupe number in the diegesis.

American critics generally responded positively. The *Los Angeles Times*, which liked the film first time around, judged the director's cut 'richer' than the original, and 'sure to be ranked as one of the key American films of the decade' (Thomas 2004). The *Village Voice* remained supportive, although with reservations about the use of the extracts from 'The Philosophy of Time Travel', which 'diminish the narrative's mystery and disrupt its somnambulist tempo' (Lim 2004). The *San Francisco Chronicle*, which gave a mixed response in 2001, suggested that the changes, which made the psychological drama 'more compelling', might not matter to 'members of the Darko cult' but might help it to find the wider audience it merited (Addiego 2004). Roger Ebert (2004), in the *Chicago Sun-Times*, appreciated the film more in his second encounter, finding the lack of narrative closure a more positive feature than was suggested in his review of the original: 'I ignored logic and responded to tone, and like it more' (although there is more narrative closure in this version). In Seattle, where the re-release was launched, an initially positive response in the *Post-Intelligencer* in 2001 was more than matched, the additional footage in the director's cut being said not to transform the film but to enrich the characters and give 'the science fiction underpinnings a stronger philosophy' while also opening the film up to alternative interpretations: 'the wonderfully weird trip leaves you with meaty questions, both metaphysical and moral, and a journey through time-space that is, if anything, even more philosophically invigorating and emotionally intense' (Axmaker 2004; original review, Nechak 2001).[17] Some of the UK critics who liked the original were less convinced. For Peter Bradshaw (2004) in the *Guardian* the emphasis was shifted away from what he found most compelling first time around, a less literal use of time travel, as metaphor for the beginnings of paranoid schizophrenia. The *Daily Telegraph* agreed, suggesting that the film worked 'at the level of mood rather than logic or plot' and was better without the added layers of explanation (Sandhu 2004).

Wider audience responses to *Donnie Darko* can be tracked through a variety of online sources, including fan-based web-sites. To include a constituency broader than just those who define themselves as fans, if only through the process of join-ing or posting to a fan-site, the main source I have consulted for this book is the 'customer reviews' section of the DVD sales entry for the film on Amazon.com, which offers a sub-stantial sample of some 900 responses.[18] The relative merits of the two versions of the film is a significant issue for many of the reviews posted since the release of the director's cut. Opinion is divided, but with the majority favouring the original by a margin of slightly more than two-to-one.[19] There is gen-eral agreement on the key difference between the two ver-sions, along much the same lines as I have suggested above: that the original is more ambiguous, the director's cut offering a more clear-cut and literal interpretation of events. Disagreement lies in whether this is seen as an improvement or an undermining of one of the key appeals of the film. For one reviewer, the director's cut is 'The Definitive Version':

> It moves the movie away from David Lynchian ambiguity and makes it, instead, what the director always intended: an airtight, completely explicable work of science fiction, one whose basic, essential storyline can be fully grasped on the first viewing. (Eric M. Van, Watertown, MA, USA, 25 January 2005)[20]

Opinions on this issue are often closely connected with conceptions of the intended viewer, a point made explicitly in some cases. As one reviewer puts it:

> I think its [sic] best to look at these two versions as separate movies for different audiences, the director's cut more suitable for mainstream American audiences and the original for people that like what mainstream Americans call 'weird' movies. (Ausar 'Music Fan', Pennsylvania, 20 February 2005)

This is put more strongly by many of those who prefer the original. Several describe the director's cut as a 'dumbing down', 'an attempt to wring a bit more cash from the film's initial cult success' (Eric M. Gregory, Virginia, USA, 25 May 2005), 'something of a "*Donnie Darko* for Dummies" version' (Sunshine Greeny, June 10, 2005); 'In short, the DC killed everything that was unique and interesting about the film and made it into a film for the masses (just to make money) (I am Jack's Name PlanetSun, Seattle, WA, USA, 1 November 2005).

Such views about the director's cut are unsurprising, looking at the entire sample of Amazon reviews, in which *Donnie Darko*'s ambiguity and scope for a range of interpretations is by far the most-cited reason for admiration of the film.[21] Confusion is, conversely, one of the sources of objection for the minority of reviewers who respond wholly or mostly negatively to the film itself, rather than any particular version (72 out of 900, or eight per cent).[22] Other negative judgements range from suggestions that the film is 'boring' to complaints that it does not live up to the 'hype' provided by sources such as the majority of extremely positive reviews posted on the Amazon site. A number of reviewers accuse fans of the film of being 'pretentious'. As one puts it: 'I resent some of these reviews where the people who loved it are calling those of us who didn't stupid for not seeing the brilliance' ('A viewer', no details provided, posted 9 February 2004). Many fans do make such distinctions, a typical formulation being the following: 'WARNING: This film is not for people who like to have their movies spoon-fed to them, who prefer not to think deeply or for narrow-minded, cultureless bores' (A. Tucker, Jacksonville, FL, 5 March 2006). Assertions of this kind are familiar currency in favourable viewer responses to films defined largely through their difference from 'mainstream' Hollywood productions, part of a process through which such products are used by consumers to make their own claims of distinction from what is perceived as 'ordinary' or 'mainstream' society. This goes to the heart of the social-cultural dimension of the consumption of cult cinema, an issue to which we will return later.

Many reviewers still find plenty of scope for interpretation and speculation in the director's cut, at the levels of both immediate narrative clarity and broader implications. The same goes for postings on more or less specialised fan-sites. A section of the '*Donnie Darko* fan-site' hosted by ProBoards devoted to questions relating to the ending was still generating new threads of questions and answers well into 2007, some three years after the release of the director's cut, many of them generating dozens of replies and viewings running into thousands.[23] The same was true of various postings to the film's 'message boards' on the Internet Movie Database.[24] This fits further with Matt Hills' definition of cult potential created by the deferral of narrative, 'a space for interpretation, speculation and fan affect which cannot be closed down by final "proof" or "fact"' (2002: 143), the latter including in this case direct interventions from the authorial source. Apart from its openness to interpretation, other grounds on which the film is widely praised by Amazon reviewers include its 'originality' and, allied with this, its success in pulling off an unconventional blend of genres. Some identify the film unproblematically with discrete genre categories, most commonly science fiction or horror but also formulations such as 'psychological thriller' or science fiction/horror hybrid. Many describe it as 'unclassifiable', however, a term usually employed with highly positive connotations. *Donnie Darko*'s ability to mix and shift across generic terrain comes across as a major source of its appeal as a departure from the Hollywood norm, although for a minority this is a ground for criticism on the basis of 'incoherence'. A number of reviewers point out that they were initially not attracted to the film because it was sold as a horror movie, some blaming the marketing campaign for its initial failure at the box office. In addition to appreciating the film as a particular kind of film industry product – one to be distinguished on such grounds from most Hollywood releases – a substantial number of Amazon reviewers also respond positively to what they take from *Donnie Darko* as its 'message', however exactly it is interpreted. Some find the film profound or disturbing, in various ways, a dimension important in many cases to its adoption as a favourite worthy of high levels of personal investment. How exactly these qualities are grounded in the text itself will be considered in the next chapter.

3

READING *DONNIE DARKO*

How, then, might *Donnie Darko* be understood in more detail? It is, clearly, a film that attracted and has continued to attract passionate engagement from a significant number of viewers, well beyond the relative few who chose or were able to see it on its initial theatrical release in the United States. Some of the reasons for its popularity among certain sectors of the audience have already been considered, and will be explored further in this chapter, along with other dimensions of the film. A number of different approaches are required if we are fully to understand both the film itself and the extent to which it lent itself to the achievement of cult status. This chapter will begin with further consideration of the way *Donnie Darko* is 'positioned' in the marketplace of popular-cultural production and consumption, including its generic status and its relationship with a range of other texts, both cinematic and otherwise. Close attention will also be paid to the formal features of the film, including dimensions such as narrative (already considered to some extent above), cinematography and the soundtrack. It will also consider how *Donnie Darko* can be understood in its social, cultural, political and historical contexts, as an early twenty-first-century revisiting of a moment in the culture and politics of the late 1980s and as a contribution to broader fictional constructions of contemporary suburban American life.

Donnie Darko is a film designed for a particular kind of market niche, despite the difficulties it experienced initially in finding its audience. In broad terms, it is clearly marked out as an 'independent' or 'indie' feature in more ways than just the industrial location outlined in chapter two. Its blending of generic conventions is one marker of this status, as are many of the formal qualities to be considered below. A typical signifier of films at the commercially-viable end of the American indie spectrum is a combination of use of and play with, or undermining of, conventional genre components (King 2005). The prominent inclusion of a 'troubled teenager' dimension suggests the primary targeting within this sector of a specific demographic, a youth audience likely to identify with the ordeal of the central character, although reference points are also included for older viewers (sympathetic parent figures, 1980s nostalgia and more general 'independent' resonances likely to attract what are understood as more mature 'discriminating' art-house audiences). Particular dimensions of the film might also be attractive to different viewers on the basis of gender. *Donnie Darko* offers a number of qualities of potential appeal to a range of viewers, defined on a number of different axes, a source of strength in some respects that can also create difficulties, commercially, when it comes to establishing a clear position in the marketplace.

GENRE AND MODALITY

Genre is a dimension key to an understanding of some of the principle qualities of the film and how these might be related to different grounds of potential audience appeal; the combination of the latter might help to explain the levels of investment the film has attracted from significant numbers of viewers. That *Donnie Darko* combines elements associated with different film genres has become a well-established part of its reputation and cult status. The list of genres cited in reference to the film usually includes science fiction, horror, teen or high school drama and/or romance and psychological thriller. It is notable that the film could be listed under all five main categories used in Timothy Shary's analysis of American youth cinema in the 1980s and 1990s (youth in schools, delinquent youth, youth horror, youth and science, youth in love and/or having sex) (Shary 2002). The establishment and combination of different generic components can be traced through the early movements of the film. The opening scenes combine impressions of mystery and suburban-teenage/family milieu. The sound of thunder plays over the company titles, continuing briefly over the first images, the camera moving in dawn light across a line of trees at the top of a ridge before finding a figure (Donnie) lying in the middle of a country road. Dark, brooding notes accompany birdsong on the soundtrack, shifting to a plangent piano theme – a more human and emotional touch – as Donnie sits up and the camera swings around him into a mid-shot. An airy, heavenly choir takes over as we are given a dawn landscape vista, a frame into which Donnie stands, a puzzled expression on his face. The overall effect is to generate a sense of mystery (what is he doing?) and hints of the otherworldly (first light as a privileged moment, the dark elements of the soundtrack, the choir). A strange transitional effect leads into the next sequence, maintaining a sense of something beyond the ordinary. A bright light seems to come out of part of the sky, whiting out the image to the accompaniment of a deep 'whoosh' on the soundtrack. Next, we see Donnie on his bicycle (in pyjamas), riding to the initial

Horror-generic hint: the Halloween carnival sign past which Donnie rides after the opening sequence

guitar twang and then lyrics of Echo and the Bunnymen's 'Killing Moon', a track that has dark resonances but the tones of which have quite a jaunty, lifting effect in this sequence. As we first see Donnie reach suburban streets, three-quarters of the screen is filled in the foreground by a hoarding advertising a Halloween carnival – a nod towards horror. A leafy, well-heeled suburban setting is established in further shots of Donnie cycling through the streets and reaching his home, where a brief moment of comic by-play is enacted between figures who will soon be identified as his father, Eddie, and elder sister, Elizabeth (Maggie Gyllenhaal).

Donnie's return home and the brief introduction of his family (continued with shots of his younger sister, Samantha (Daveigh Chase), on a trampoline and his mother, Rose (Mary McDonnell), reading Stephen King's *It* – another horror-related hint) is followed by a dinner-table scene. This is a conventional routine in the teen/family drama, achieved through some pointed exchanges of dialogue, establishing a context of sibling rivalry and other family tensions including the fact that Donnie is in therapy and has not been taking his medication. It is followed by a hostile encounter between Donnie and his mother (including her question 'where do you go at night?', which sustains that element of mystery), a subsequent moment between the two parents and a sequence in which the father wakes and goes downstairs to watch televised exchanges between presidential rivals Michael Dukakis and George Bush Sr. The camera closes in on a clock reading midnight – another signifier of the otherworldly, the 'witching hour'. It is at this point, some eight minutes in, that a more explicit horror or dark fantasy dimension is first introduced. A deep, unearthly voice issues the instruction to 'wake up' as we shift to Donnie's room and a sequence accompanied by dark, brooding undertones on the soundtrack, further signifiers of the presence of some unspecified supernatural presence. Donnie, apparently in a trance, is led outside the house and we are introduced to the figure in the rabbit suit later identified as Frank. The various dark or beyond-the-usual resonances previously offered by the film are at this point literalised and made concrete in this figure, the design of which somewhat incongruously mixes the qualities of a furry animal suit and its more horror-inclined mask. '28 days, six hours, 42 minutes, 12 seconds', Frank intones: 'That is when the world will end', the first suggestion of a specific fantasy/supernatural/apocalyptic agenda.

What follows gives this some concrete foundation, although its meaning remains far from clear to the uninitiated viewer. Images of Eddie Darko asleep in front of television static and Elizabeth returning home from a night out are followed by a major soundtrack jolt that proves to be the impact of a jet engine falling on the house. Donnie returns to the scene, having been found asleep on a golf course, and it is revealed that the engine fell into his room (it is clear that it would have killed him, and therefore that Frank saved his life). The general sense of mystery is deepened when it is revealed that the 'experts' do not know where the engine came from, a fact that increases the extent to which a supernatural dimension appears to be in play, and an element of conspiracy thriller is also suggested by the generally sinister nature of the Federal Aviation Administration officialdom with which the Darko family engages. The film then enacts a clear shift of generic territory, into the 'high school' format, for a series of exchanges on the way to and at the school attended by Donnie – these include the introduction of what appear to be a number of stock characters such as the school bully, the principal and positively- and negatively-coded teachers. Another dose of the horror/supernatural comes some 25 minutes into the film, when Donnie is led by Frank to flood the school, an incident that includes the physically inexplicable lodging of an axe in the head of a statue. Teen romance comes into the picture when, as a result of the flood and the cancellation of lessons, Donnie establishes a relationship with Gretchen. The mixture of these elements continues in this fashion until another ingredient is introduced when Frank, in a further exchange with Donnie, raises the issue of time travel, a subject usually associated with science fiction. This is given greater elaboration (and some grounding in theoretical physics via reference to Stephen Hawking) in discussion between Donnie and science teacher Monnitoff and the latter's gift of a copy of Roberta Sparrow's 'The Philosophy of Time Travel'. By

Donnie and Gretchen embrace, in the teen-romance component of the film

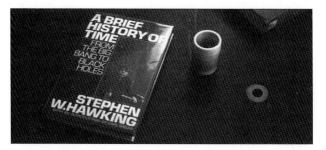

Science fact/fiction introduced to the generic mix, via Stephen Hawking

this stage, the principal generic ingredients are all in place. The elements of horror and science fiction lend themselves particularly to the potential acquisition of cult status, as two genres the extraordinary dimensions of which have led to their disproportionate representation in the cult canon. We have also seen Donnie during his therapy sessions with Dr Thurman. These, along with other indications of Donnie's troubled state of mind, provide a basis for the reading according to which the fantasy elements are interpreted as products solely or primarily of his consciousness.

To better understand exactly how *Donnie Darko* mixes these different components it is useful to move from genre to the concept of *modality*, a broader way of analysing the manner in which specific elements of the film are presented both within and across particular generic territories. The term, as used by Robert Hodge and David Tripp, suggests different ways of 'situating messages in relation to an ostensible reality' (1986: 43). All texts contain modality markers, devices that position them in some way in terms of the kinds of claims they make in relation to an understanding of the real world. News or documentary footage, for example, deploys conventions that make claims to the status of representing the actual events of an identifiable exterior world.

The same can be said, although to a lesser extent, of material presented as 'serious' drama. In this case, the material will be fictional, an invented story, but presented in a manner that claims some significant resonance with equivalents in the known real world. Some genres include signifiers that make clear that their defining materials are less closely related to the stuff of the real world (it is important to note that this is a question of *relative* degrees rather than absolute distinctions). Fantasy genres usually include signifiers that underline the unreal (or, at the very least, questionable or speculative) status of key dimensions of their fictional universes. Once a text is marked as unambiguously in the realm of horror, science fiction or fantasy (in various ways, ranging from titles and marketing to plot material), the viewer is encouraged to accept a frame of reference at least partially different from that applied to avowedly more 'realistic' fictions. Events such as irruptions from other dimensions or time travel are *expected* as part of the established generic repertoire in horror and science fiction, for example, but not usually in the troubled-teen or teen/family-tensions drama. The striking quality of *Donnie Darko* lies in its mixture of modalities as much as, or perhaps more than and underlying, its blend of genres.

The horror and science fiction dimensions create a potential for the material to be relatively more distanced from viewers, because they entail the acceptance of a situation beyond that of any known possibility in the world they occupy. The emotional-dramatic dimensions of the film, associated primarily with other generic components, counter this effect, creating potential for a greater sense of what Susan Purdie (1993) terms 'implication' in the material on screen: encouragement for the viewer to sympathise or empathise with the characters and to treat the events represented on screen as 'real' within the fictional frame. Most horror or science fiction films also seek to create this kind of viewer implication; the potency of a horror film lies to a large extent in the degree to which the viewer is encouraged to share, vicariously, the terrifying experiences faced by central characters. The difference is that this is usually done within a frame that brackets off the experience as not applicable in any literal sense to anything very close to the real world occupied by the viewer. A strong sense of 'psychological' or 'emotional' realism might be offered as an important part of the experience and pleasure of the form in many such examples – an evocation of the reaction that might be expected if fantastic events did come to pass – but this is likely to be bracketed (more than would otherwise be the case) by the generic barrier.[25] *Donnie Darko* achieves much of its depth and resonance precisely by blurring such lines to a greater extent than usual (again, the difference is relative rather than absolute, an important qualification if oversimplification is to be avoided) and increasing the overall implication quotient on offer. (Whether or not such invitations to sympathy/empathy are taken up by all viewers is another question; it is always possible for viewers to refuse the offer and to remain more distanced, as is clearly the case with some of the detractors in the Amazon sample considered in the previous chapter.) The emotional drama of the film, rooted mostly in its use of the troubled-teenager/ family-drama components, is not dissipated by the fantastic elements, as can sometimes be the case, but tends to underpin the whole work. This is especially true of the original edition, in which the fantasy dimension is most closely cross-wired with the more realistically-grounded evocation of the troubled teenager and his family context. The result is that the film generates a mood of dread and anxiety that might be rooted in specific objects and events, such as the appearance of Frank and the threatened apocalypse, but that also spreads more widely through the texture of the piece.[26] In this respect, *Donnie Darko* fits quite well into Tzvetan Todorov's much-cited definition of the 'fantastic' in fiction as involving hesitation on the part of the reader/viewer (and, in some cases, on the part of the central character) between natural and supernatural explanations of diegetic events (1975: 25). The norm, for Todorov, is for this hesitation eventually to be resolved one way or the other, although his formulation allows for the existence of distinctive texts such as *Donnie Darko* (or a literary example such as the Henry James tale 'The Turn of the Screw', adapted on film as *The Innocents* (1961)) in which the ambiguity can be sustained beyond the end of the narrative.

The simultaneous presence of the two dimensions is clearest in two sequences involving Donnie's sessions with his therapist, Dr Thurman. The first provides a combination of expert diagnosis, leaning strongly towards 'explaining away' Donnie's experiences as the result of psychosis, and imagery that presents us with their apparent 'reality' on screen. Donnie's aggressive behaviour and increasing detachment from reality 'seem to stem from his inability to cope with the forces in the world that he perceives as threatening', Dr Thurman tells his parents. She describes his encounters with Frank as 'a daylight hallucination', 'a common occurrence among paranoid schizophrenics'. At the same time we are shown one of these experiences – Donnie using a kitchen knife in an attempt to break through the barrier that separates the two dimensions in which he and Frank are located. As in the scenes from the trailer discussed in chapter two, what is partially a sound/image hierarchy might apply here in which what we see with our own eyes of Donnie's experience (see and hear, in fact) is likely to override Thurman's diagnosis. It is also a familiar generic convention, if the appropriate genre is in play during this sequence, that secular 'experts' fail to appreciate the supernatural experiences of characters in films such as this. The emotional resonances of the scene

Inviting emotional engagement: Donnie during one of his sessions with Dr Thurman

between Thurman and Donnie's parents play across the boundary, however, giving added depth and potency to the human level of emotional engagement/implication offered by the film as a whole. Rose, in particular, is not just a negative-reference-point parental figure, but written and played as a rounded character whose concerns we are invited to share (the same applies to Eddie, although his key bonding scene with his son was cut from the original version). Much the same kind of emotional realism surrounds Donnie's plight, again a combination of the way it is written and the perfor-mance by Gyllenhaal. This is to the fore in a second encounter with Thurman. Under hypnosis, Donnie admits to flooding the school and setting fire to Jim Cunningham's home, going on to talk about time machines and a future in which Frank is go-ing to kill and the sky is going to open up. He can see Frank right now, he says, as we, too, see the figure manifested on the screen. The sequence offers further reinforcement of the fantastic, time travel-based narrative but closely interwoven with the sympathetic emotional drama of a seriously troubled youth. And Donnie is troubled, and invites emotional engage-ment, *either way*: as a teenager suffering from schizophrenic hallucinations or one with world-saving duties imposed upon his daily routine; or as one unsure himself which is really the case.

The capacity for *Donnie Darko*'s fantasy plot to be read as a metaphor for a more prosaic teenage crisis is undoubtedly one of the sources of the film's resonance with many viewers. For those who are currently undergoing or have recently experienced such difficulties, he offers a strong point of emotional allegiance. The fantasy dimension might be read, from this perspective, as an objective correlative of the problems of adolescence, an imaginary scenario sufficient to give expression to the larger-than-life subjective experience of generational angst, and to appeal on that basis to some viewers. The same might be said of many teen-oriented horror and/or fantasy products, the difference in the case of *Donnie Darko* being the sustained manner (especially in the original version) in which the more 'ordinary' dimension is kept at the forefront, rather than being lost or relegated amid the enactment of more formulaic/generic routines.[27] The fantasy dimension of *Donnie Darko* is sufficiently anchored in the day-to-day business of teenage alienation to serve such a function while keeping relatively open the question of the ultimate nature or reality of the extraordinary elements of his experience. This provides a strong basis of appeal for an audience defined by relative youth, the same constituency also likely to be attracted in part by the fantasy/horror/science fiction generic components. *Donnie Darko* fits here with the suggestion by J. P. Telotte that the primary audience for the midnight movie variety of cult film falls into 'the 17-to-24-year-old group that often – as a sort of rite of passage – sees itself as separate from the cultural mainstream', a process towards which the consumption of such works might contribute (1991a: 10). The mixture of modalities and generic inheritances also gives the film potential to appeal across gender lines. Horror, science fiction and fantasy are generally associated primarily with the preferences of male audiences. Family drama and teenage romance might be expected to appeal more particularly to a female constituency. A perception of *Donnie Darko* as more than usually heartfelt is certainly a feature of a considerable number of the Amazon customer reviews and appears to be an important source in this case of the kind of fan attachment that contributes to the achievement of cult status. Many respondents, here and in other forums, were able to draw connections between the film and their own emotional experiences, as was also the case with fans who provided feedback – in some cases, lengthy – to the British distributor, Metrodome, as part of a competition to select interview subjects for one of the features accompanying the director's cut DVD.[28]

INTERTEXTS

In addition to its generic inheritances, *Donnie Darko* is also situated in the context of a range of more specific or individual intertextual sources, literary and cinematic. Some are cited explicitly, within the text, while others provide implicit resonances that might be of greater or lesser relevance depending on their familiarity to the viewer. They all contribute, potentially, to the process of locating the film in its wider cultural and cinematic context and creating potential for investment and debate on the part of *Donnie Darko* enthusiasts. Explicit reference is made to the films *The Evil Dead* (1981), *Back to the Future* (1985) and, to a lesser extent, *The Last Temptation of Christ* (1988). Literary texts cited directly in the film are the Graham Greene story 'The Destructors', *Watership Down* (1972) by Richard Adams, cited in the director's cut only, and Stephen King's *It* (1986). The relevance of these sources to the material of *Donnie Darko* is variable, including in some cases the establishment of the 1980s setting, although the choice by the filmmaker to insert them into the film can be taken as an invitation to read them as offering some form of direct connection or commentary. In the case of *Back to the Future*, a time travel fantasy involving a teenager as the central character, the relationship is immediately obvious, the film being cited approvingly by Donnie during a conversation with Monnitoff about time travel. The inclusion of scenes from *The Evil Dead*, in a sequence in which Donnie is visited by Frank during a midnight movie screening, is a display of cult movie credentials on the part of the film, a self-conscious gesture towards the kind of status to which *Donnie Darko* might have aspired and eventually achieved in the same type of venue. Accompanying *The Evil Dead* on the bill but not attended by Donnie and seen only in title on the marquee is *The Last Temptation of Christ*. In this case, the reference is passing and requires much more work on the part of the viewer if it is to be mobilised in relation to a reading of the film. Such a reading is very possible, however, via interpretations of *Donnie Darko* in the context of Christian theology, an issue to which we return below.

'The Destructors' is the secondary text most explicitly cited in the film, a story being taught in Donnie's English class and the subject of controversy when its influence is blamed for the flooding of the school. A degree of parallel is implied between Donnie and the central character of the story, who leads a group of youths in the systematic destruction of the home of a character known as Old Misery. 'The Destructors' shares with *Donnie Darko* an ability to generate uncertainty at the level of tone. It can be read ironically, as Donnie suggests in class, a dimension entirely missed by the self-appointed moral guardian of the school, Kitty Farmer, who succeeds in getting it removed from the curriculum. The point of the story is that the destruction is enacted largely for its own sake, coldly and methodically, out of no sense of

'Destruction is a form of creation': Donnie gives his reading of 'The Destructors'

hatred for Old Misery and for no gain (other than at the level of repute). The final note is one of comedy, in the reaction of a truck driver who unwittingly completes the process of bringing down the house, leaving the story in a state of uncertain modality, if rather different from that of the film. The effect of the story's initial deployment in *Donnie Darko* is to give added resonance to some of the early plot events. Karen Pomeroy reads an extract to Donnie's class, a passage (slightly edited) that includes mention of the protagonist's 'pain of puberty' in his fifteenth year. The line implies a connection with Donnie (a link made more explicit in the trailer). Asked for his opinion on the story following his recent 'brush with mass destruction' (a reference to the jet engine crashing into his room and an overt invitation for us to make a connection between the story and film), Donnie's interpretation is that for the protagonists 'destruction is a form of creation … They just want to see what happens when they tear the world apart. They want to change things.'

How this plays at this stage of the film depends on the state of the viewer's knowledge of what is to come and/or of the parallel-universe backstory. For the uninitiated viewer (that is, most viewers on first watching), it provides a broad layering of additional semantic texture, a sense that some meaning underlies the instances of destruction witnessed in the early stages of the film: the jet engine crash and Donnie's flooding of the school. In the case of the latter, particularly, it contributes a positive connotation, implying that it is more than an act of vandalism, as will prove to be the case (the flood ensures the closure of the school that, in turn, brings Donnie and Gretchen together that morning, thus setting in train a key component of the process that leads Donnie to save the world). In any dispute over the reality or otherwise of the supernatural dimension of *Donnie Darko*, the citation of 'The Destructors' and Donnie's reading of the text might also be taken as evidence for the non-literal interpretation, however. Read more closely in line with 'The Destructors', some of Donnie's actions might be interpreted as arbitrary, ironic and perhaps even existentialist, as expressing a rebellious desire to 'tear the world apart', 'to change things' – for its own sake, as a marker of his own ability to act upon the world, rather than as part of any external metaphysical scheme.

In the director's cut, it is made clear that 'The Destructors' is replaced in the school's English curriculum by *Watership Down*, an extract from the animated film of which is shown being screened to Donnie's class before a discussion of the text. Aspects of *Watership Down* can also be read into *Donnie Darko*, particularly the extraordinary ability of one of the rabbit characters, Fiver, to pick up intimations of disaster. A 'terrible thing is coming', Fiver is heard to say in the extract shown to the class, one of the numerous hints added to the director's cut. That Donnie, too, is unusually sensitive and picks up general impressions that something is amiss in his world is a point emphasised in Kelly's DVD commentary on the original version. Pomeroy makes a comment during discussion of the book about 'the miracle of storytelling' that also seems applicable to *Donnie Darko* itself, referring to the 'dea ex machina, the god machine. That's what saved the rabbits.' Something similar could be said of the forces manipulating Donnie in the film, the potential religious connotations of which will be considered below (there is a literal *dea ex machina* in *Watership Down*, in the understanding of the rabbits, a car used to take the injured central character Hazel to safety towards the end of the book; the expression seems less applicable than Pomeroy appears to suggest to the ability of Fiver to see into what might be a parallel world of dreams, a world that resonates with the alternative dimensions of *Donnie Darko*).

The presence of *Watership Down* in the narrative also operates at the level of a self-referential in-joke, of course, given the rabbit connection with the form in which Frank appears to Donnie (the background presence of such material is a familiar movie convention; the film also includes numerous rabbit toys and other such references in its marginal detail). Another reference to which attention has often been drawn on this level is *Harvey* (1950), which features a 6ft 3½in rabbit described as a mischievous fairy spirit and visible only to the central character, Elwood P. Dowd (James Stewart). Richard Kelly maintains that he had not seen *Harvey* before making *Donnie Darko*, but there are some points of similarity between the two, beyond the presence of a large rabbit figure and the very different tones of the two films (*Harvey* is a gentle, benign fantasy). Harvey, unseen by the viewer, can be taken as real or imaginary. Grounds for the latter exist in Dowd's constant propensity to drink martinis, the former being suggested more strongly by a number of acts of mischief attributable to the spirit and the eventual acceptance of its reality by other characters. Much as in *Donnie Darko*, Harvey's presence is ascribed by psychological experts to 'third-degree hallucination', while according to Dowd his powers include the ability to stop time.

The rabbit form taken by Frank also brings with it a range of wider intertextual and cultural associations. The most obviously applicable to *Donnie Darko* is from Lewis Carroll's *Alice's Adventures in Wonderland* (1865), the alternative universe of which is reached by a trip 'down the rabbit-hole', a phrase that has gained wider usage to imply a shift into other dimensions (as employed, for example, in *The Matrix* (1999)). A number of more specific parallels can be suggested between the rabbit figures of *Donnie Darko* and *Alice's Adventures in Wonderland*. A sleepy Alice sees a white rabbit, runs after it across a field and follows it down the hole. Donnie is wakened by a figure in a rabbit suit and follows it to a nearby golf course (with its own holes). The white rabbit acts as Alice's guide in the strange world underground, just as Frank guides the course of Donnie's actions in the Tangent Universe.[29] The sequence in which Donnie seeks to break through the watery barrier between his and Frank's dimensions also carries echoes of Carroll's sequel, *Through the Looking Glass* (1872), another trope that has entered into the culture, although with the difference that Donnie is not looking into a mirror (the barrier appears opposite the mirror in his bathroom) or able to cross into the other side. Beyond specific texts of this kind, the rabbit or the hare has a number of symbolic resonances in Western and other cultures, most notably in this context an association with spring, life and rebirth.[30]

Donnie Darko also resonates with a number of films that explore aspects of time travel or that blur the lines between present-life and the worlds of death, dreams and alternate realities. Films cited in the Amazon sample considered in the previous chapter include *Jacob's Ladder* (1990), *Twelve Monkeys* (1995), *Vanilla Sky* (2001) and *The Butterfly Effect* (2004). *Twelve Monkeys*, 'inspired by' Chris Marker's *La Jetée* (1962), revolves around a 'divergent realities' mechanism similar in some respects to that of *Donnie Darko*. The central character, Cole (Bruce Willis), is sent back into the past from 2035 to try to avert an apocalyptic outbreak of disease. In the past, 1990, his claims that much of humanity will be wiped out by a deadly virus in 1997 are taken as the ramblings of a madman. At one point he comes to doubt his own sanity, suffering from the confusion of attempting to live simultaneously in two different dimensions. He eventually sacrifices himself in an effort to kill a scientist who plans to release the virus although, unlike Donnie, he fails in the attempt. *Jacob's Ladder* and *Vanilla Sky* (the latter released two months after Kelly's film) have central plot devices similar to the reading of *Donnie Darko* according to which the main body of the film is understood as having been dreamt by Donnie in the hours immediately preceding the crash of the jet engine. The protagonist of each turns out to be dead and narrative events to have been either dreamt or to occupy some ambiguous hallucinatory dimension. *The Butterfly Effect*, although released three years after *Donnie Darko,* occupies similar territory, joining such films in what might be seen as a dreamt/alternative-reality cycle. Other contemporary films that play with life/death status in some similar ways include *The Sixth Sense* (1999) and *The Others* (2001) where the existential status of central characters proves to be other than initally portrayed. Much the same can be said of the latter part of *The Last Temptation of Christ*, one of the films directly referenced in *Donnie Darko*, in which Christ (Willem Dafoe) experiences a parallel-narrative/dream existence in which he is reprieved on the cross and leads a secular family life until he is reawakened and returned on discovering that it has been the work of the Devil.

An earlier source for such rug-pulling endings is Ambrose Bierce's tale 'An Occurrence at Owl Creek Bridge' (1891), an American Civil War story about a man's apparent escape from execution by hanging, which turns out to a dream/fantasy occupying the last moments of his life; a French film version of the story, *La Rivière du Hibou* (1962), broadcast as part of the *Twilight Zone* series in the US, has been cited by Kelly in several interviews as an influence on the climax of *Donnie Darko*. Another example, sharing the potential ambiguity of *Donnie Darko* but unfolding in the long, slow sequences of a work clearly located at the art-cinema end of the spectrum, is Andrei Tarkovsky's *The Sacrifice* (1986). The central character makes a pact with God, agreeing to give up everything he loves if the consequences of an imminent nuclear war can be averted. He wakes the next morning to find the world apparently returned to normal and follows through on his commitment, burning down his beloved house by the sea and being taken away from his family to an institution, the dream or reality status of the previous threat being left open to question. Most of these examples offer eventual resolution, however, relying on the frissons provided by late plot twists and shock revelations more than sustained hesitation between different interpretations, an effect closer to that offered by the director's cut than by the original version of *Donnie Darko*.[31]

Parallel universes of the 'what would have happened if…' variety are also central to the *Back to the Future* trilogy (1985, 1989, 1990) and the Frank Capra classic *It's a Wonderful Life* (1946), the latter drawn upon very clearly in *Back to the Future Part II* and often cited in relation to *Donnie Darko*. Kelly offers a darker and reversed version of *It's a Wonderful Life*. Donnie dies, apparently, to save those around him (not to mention the universe as a whole), while Capra's despairing protagonist, George Bailey (James Stewart), is convinced *not* to kill himself after being given a nightmare vision of the world as it would have turned out if he had never been born. *Back to the Future Part II* offers a more playful take on similar material, the small-town setting becoming seedy and violent in a parallel existence in which the time travelling car invented by

Doc Brown (Christopher Lloyd) is appropriated by the series' villain. Biff Tanen (Thomas F. Wilson). *Donnie Darko*, in Kelly's reading, is founded on a 'straight' and serious treatment of time travel lore that is played for laughs in the *Back to the Future* sequel. Disastrous consequences might result from one character, travelling into the future, meeting her future self, warns the Doc. It could cause a time paradox the result of which might be a chain reaction that would unravel the fabric of the space-time continuum and – as threatened in *Donnie Darko* – destroy the entire universe; but it might not, he adds, which in this clearly comic territory proves to be correct.

The modality of *Donnie Darko* is generally dark, brooding and serious, with some moments of comic relief (notably the delayed revelation of Donnie's suggestion to Farmer where to shove her 'Lifeline' exercise card). The presence of a variety of intertexts contributes to the dominant tone in many respects. Where they might be recognised as such, however, references to other texts can have a distancing effect, highlighting the fictional nature of the film along with the other works to which attention is drawn. To make the viewer aware of parallel situations in 'The Destructors' or *Watership Down* is potentially to bring to attention the constructed nature of all such texts, especially when overt reference is made to 'the miracle of storytelling', as in Pomeroy's comment about the latter in the director's cut. The existence of these texts within the primary narrative is realistically motivated: they are the kinds of works we might expect Donnie and his classmates to be studying in their English class. But they are also *excessively* applicable to the film's own narrative matter to be guaranteed entirely to disappear into the fabric of the fictional world, even if the presence of such implicitly reflective background material has become a widely established cinematic device. The same could be said of the presence of

The Evil Dead, a plausible choice of viewing for Donnie but one that is also, for those familiar with the film, rather overt and potentially intrusive in its status as a marked signifier of cult horror.

References such as these can contribute to the modality status of a film, indicating a basis in the particular universe of cinema-as-construct in addition to any claims made to a closer relationship with the extra-cinematic 'real' world. The balance of emphasis is variable. The work of Quentin Tarantino might be located at one extreme, often favouring what Tarantino terms the 'movie, movie' world, one in which a primary ground of reference is an array of existing film and other popular-cultural products. *Donnie Darko* fits into a broader territory in which such citations generally play a less central role, although generic points of reference are also an important part of this equation: the overt mixing of genres, widely seen as one of the film's strengths, also has the potential to draw attention to its own status as a particular kind of cultural confection. A number of additional movie references can also be detected in *Donnie Darko*, including implicit nods towards *E.T. The Extra-Terrestrial* (1982) (Donnie and friends cycling off on a mission towards the end, homage to both the role of Drew Barrymore in the production and Kelly's fondness for the film and Spielberg's work in general) and *Halloween* (1978) (in the setting of the climax and details such as the Halloween celebration poster seen in the early stages). For the writer-director this is to a large extent a matter of paying dues to sources, influences or favourite works. Another example is the background presence of Stephen King's *It*, a generic marker-point, but also a tribute to a writer Kelly credits with teaching him the art of creating fantasy worlds and suspense (Scott 2003: xiv). Specific references to *It* can also be suggested, including the role played by cellars as routes into the world of supernatural presence, even if this is a common horror trope, and the clown costume worn by Frank's passenger in the car that kills Gretchen, similar to the garb with which King's evil presence is most frequently associated.[32] Kelly also pays homage to Stanley Kubrick's *Lolita* (1962), a film he showed to the crew as a tonal reference (for 'its absurdist humour and pathos' (in Scott 2003: xxxviii–xl)), in the costume worn by Elizabeth to the Halloween party and the style of the footlights in the Sparkle Motion performance.[33]

NARRATIVE

The narrative ambiguity of *Donnie Darko* is a dimension in which the film has been situated in relation to a number of other productions from similar regions of the American film landscape (either independent or in the 'Indiewood' territory where the independent and Hollywood sectors overlap). On this level and in terms of its overall tone, its mixture of the dark and the quirky, *Donnie Darko* has been likened to the work of David Lynch, particularly *Lost Highway* (1997) and *Mulholland Dr.* It is in this connection that we turn to consideration of the formal qualities of the film. *Donnie Darko* shares with *Mulholland Dr.*, and some of the other examples cited above, the introduction of a climactic twist that throws into question the status of much or all that has gone before. Unlike relatively more conventional examples, *Mulholland Dr.* invites confusion rather than manifesting a simple change of state, the most plausible hypothesis being that the narrative has been an elaborate fantasy generated from the envy of one of the central characters. Very like *Donnie Darko*, the film generated much speculation, and not a little frustration, among viewers, a quality exploited by a promotional campaign that suggested it needed to be seen more than once. Similar reactions were provoked by *Lost Highway*, in which a major narrative reversal is created midway through the film, a central character being transformed into an entirely different person for reasons that are never anything other than deeply enigmatic. This kind of subversion of narrative convention is motivated in these examples partly by the qualities associated with the director; the pleasure offered by *Lost Highway* and *Mulholland Dr.* is, as I have suggested elsewhere, to some extent the pleasure precisely of Lynchian ambiguity and enigma (King 2005: 101). *Mulholland Dr.* is one of the films most frequently cited in the Amazon sample, usually in the context of viewers recommending *Donnie Darko* to those who liked *Mulholland Dr.*, or having had the film recommended to them on the same basis. For large numbers of the Amazon respondents, though, *Donnie Darko* is a film to be interpreted and resolved, as far as possible, rather than enjoyed specifically for its ambiguity, even if many are happy to accept the existence of a plurality of readings. It is a film characterised by the demand it sets for more than average narrative *work* on the part of the viewer, if its broader narrative arc is to be comprehended to any substantial extent (whichever particular interpretation is made). It joins, in this respect, a group of contemporary films the 'independent' status of which is marked formally by departure from the more immediately transparent norms usually associated with 'classical' Hollywood narrative design (other examples include *Memento*, also cited in some of the *Donnie Darko* Amazon reviews) (King 2005: 84–104).

How far *Donnie Darko* departs from the norms of Hollywood depends on the version watched and the context of viewing. The original cut, taken in isolation, remains highly enigmatic. Much is clarified if outside aides such as the website are used, but such a requirement is very much against the Hollywood norm. Hollywood narrative, or the broadly classical form used more widely, as in many independent features, is meant to be self-sufficient as far as key points of plot information are concerned. It is a marker of difference or distinction for this not to be the case, and a potential source of cult adoption. The relative lack of clarity on some key issues is encouragement to the kind of additional viewer investment that often contributes to the achievement of such status, including multiple viewings and access to DVD commentary tracks (although, for some published critics and negative postings to internet sites, the film's lack of self-sufficiency is evidence of narrative failure). Films of greater-than-average narrative complexity, ambiguity and irresolution, or those that offer final twists that throw the status of earlier events into doubt, lend themselves particularly well to an economy of repeat or multiple viewing, as confirmed by viewer research conducted by Barbara Klinger (2006: 157).[34] How, then, does the original read, at the level of the establishment and resolution or otherwise of enigmas? It is entirely usual for mainstream/ conventional films to contain narrative enigmas, particularly when the early tone constructs a dimension of 'mystery' as one of the central ingredients, as is the case with *Donnie Darko*. 'Classical' narrative structure often proceeds through a process in which enigmas are successively established and resolved, the exact balance depending on the generic or other territory involved. *Donnie Darko* abides by this pattern to a considerable extent, even in its original incarnation; it is important, here and elsewhere, to pay due heed to the conventional aspects of the film as well as its more eye-catching or attention-grabbing departures.

A central question posed at the start of the film is 'where does Donnie go at night?', or, perhaps more strongly, 'why does he go there, wherever it is?' We first see him appearing to wake on a road in the hills. As he returns home, the question is put directly in a note attached to the fridge in the family kitchen: 'Where is Donnie?' Rose repeats the question, suggesting that his nocturnal absence is a regular event, not just a one-off. We get an answer in the sequence in which we

An explicit posing of part of the narrative enigma in the note provided on the Darko fridge

first see him woken and visited by Frank: he goes, on this occasion at least, at the behest of a figure in a scary-faced rabbit suit. Characteristically, as this sequence proceeds, more questions are raised than answered: who or what is this figure and where does it come from? A countdown to 'the end of the world' is suggested by Frank, an answer of sorts to what this visitation is about, and the provision of the kind of deadline structure typical of many classical-type narratives, but this only deepens the larger enigma: what is really *going on* here; why should the end of the world be threatened; and why should Donnie be involved (other than in his basic structural role as a movie protagonist by definition likely to be involved in any such strange happenings that might occur in the film)? The glaring enigma of the jet engine follows, encouraging the viewer to make some connection between this and the business with Frank, especially as the latter appears to have saved Donnie's life. Expectations are set for an explanation of both, and of the connection between the two. Donnie's sessions with Dr Thurman put into play the alternative possibility that some of these events are imaginary and not to be resolved other than as manifestations of his troubled psyche, although his dialogues with Thurman also provide an opportunity for the repetition or further elaboration of material coming from Frank. Why Frank should urge Donnie to flood his school only adds to existing unanswered questions.

Frank's subsequent mention of time travel is deployed in a manner that suggests the provision of an important clue. Donnie's discussion of the subject with Monnitoff gives it some more concrete basis, if only at the speculative end of theoretical physics. Time travel is established as a major source of potential answers to the larger enigma, further elaborated via discussion related to 'The Philosophy of Time Travel', but exactly why remains opaque. It gradually becomes apparent, as the film advances, that Donnie has some task to perform, that it involves time travel and is designed to avert the end of the world (unless all this is dismissed as dream or hallucination). Why, though, remains almost entirely unclear, without external sources or access to deleted scenes or the director's cut. The viewer learns that a mortal-seeming figure occupies the rabbit suit, in the sequence at the midnight movie when Frank removes his mask. The enigma of his identity is resolved on one level when he is revealed as the driver of the car that kills Gretchen, the rabbit outfit being explained away at this point as a Halloween costume. Why Donnie should then shoot him in the eye is mystifying, however. It explains the eye injury witnessed in the movie theatre, but that immediately raises questions of time and causality. Unanswered, again, is the larger question: why exactly has Frank been appearing to Donnie, even if it is understood that time travel and some kind of other dimension are involved.

The moment when Rose is seen on a plane returning from the Sparkle Motion performance in Los Angeles is one of the few examples in the original cut in which overt interpretive direction is offered to the viewer (in this case, removed from the director's cut). Echoes of Donnie and Monnitoff's exchange about time travel are played over the sequence, including the latter's remark that 'a metal craft of any kind' [that is, this plane] would be suitable. That the aircraft is to be central to the time travel strand is made clear, as it suffers a major jolt and an engine is seen falling in long shot from a sky filled with unusual cloud formations of the kind recently seen above the Darko house. A cut back to Donnie getting into the family car with the body of Gretchen is overlaid with her earlier words 'what if you could go back in time and take all those hours of pain and darkness and replace them with something better' (originally spoken in relation to the 'Infant Memory Generator' imagined by herself and Donnie as part of a science project). The camera moves in close to Donnie's face, followed by a cut to an image of the jet engine falling down a semi-transparent tube through the clouds (marked quite clearly, on the basis of previous information, as a time travel portal). The screen whites-out and a series of brief fast-motion images (the perspective of the driver of a car moving down a country road; leaves against a sky; cloud shadows over a wooded hillside; clouds against a darkening sky) leads into a montage sequence in which a number of scenes from the film are replayed rapidly in reverse, suggesting an un-winding of the events so far (a more overtly science fiction impression is created in the director's cut, in which the re-verse footage is overlaid with grid lines and other audio-visual elements, including the flashing word 'purge' as the rewind begins, which creates the impression that it is a technologi-cally-based process, as suggested in the term 'god *machine*'). Over this sequence plays Donnie's voice, reading the text of a letter he has written to Roberta Sparrow, closing enigmati-cally with 'I hope that when the world comes to an end I can breathe a sigh of relief because there will be so much to look forward to.' It ends with Donnie laughing in bed, static on the television downstairs, a re-run of Elizabeth's arrival home

The imposition of grid lines and text gives a more overtly science fiction impression to the climactic reversed-footage sequence in the director's cut

from a date, Donnie smiling, the impact through the house of the jet engine, and Donnie's evident death, followed by the 'Mad World' sequence discussed in the previous chapter. It is established quite clearly that a reversal of time has somehow been effected, but the film ends with the larger 'how' and 'why' questions still persistently unresolved. The most obvious answer to the latter is that Donnie has acted, in the end, to save Gretchen, but the larger purpose for which this is only a device, in the fully elaborated backstory, is unexplained.

The original version can be read as a film that conforms in general to classical narrative conventions, but from which certain key sources of information have been withheld. What might otherwise be a relatively normal balance of enigma and enigma-resolution is offered (with plenty of scope for further interpretation, to be considered below), but with a few important explanatory scenes missing. This becomes more apparent when deleted scenes are made available on the DVD release and in many cases restored in the director's cut (some additional dialogue hints, not included in either version, are found in the published version of the script, suggesting an original intention to be somewhat more explicit, although not including any content from 'The Philosophy of Time Travel'). From this perspective, the latter version makes sense as a director's cut, as something closer to the 'true, originally-intended version' that the term usually implies. The original might be judged to be 'flawed', in classical terms, the pressure to keep down the running time appearing to have contributed to a sacrifice of narrative clarity. This is precisely what creates a key part of the film's most distinctive cult or niche-market appeal, however, and was according to Kelly part of the original intention to some extent at least (thus complicating any notion of one or the other having any privileged status as the authorial vision). It is notable that in his DVD commentary on the director's cut, Kelly adopts a musical analogy to describe it as an 'extended remix' rather than a definitive version.

Many hints of the bigger picture are given in the original version, including the use of some of the intertextual references considered above, but these are often far from easy to pick up, especially on a first or single viewing. When what will prove to be Frank's car is seen speeding towards the climactic scene outside Roberta Sparrow's house, for example, Donnie is asked by his assailant, Seth (Alex Greeenwald), if he called the cops. 'It's a *dea ex machina*', replies Donnie. In the director's cut, this echoes the term used by Pomeroy in relation to *Watership Down* and is a major clue. It is not easy to hear, however, even if the viewer is sufficiently alert to have made the connection, Donnie's voice being constrained as he pinned to the ground with a knife at his throat. Not even Seth, in close proximity, catches what he says, and it is considerably less likely to be picked up in the original version in which no prior reference to the term has been made. 'Our saviour', adds Donnie. This makes perfect sense to the viewer equipped with all the background, but otherwise is likely to seem oddly disjunctive, as the car swerves to avoid Sparrow and drives over and kills Gretchen (a moment marked as 'shocking' and impactful in the diegesis).

A more immediate hint is given in the use of the term 'cellar door'. In the full director's cut/commentary interpretation, the term is one of the numerous sources of guidance provided to Donnie in the fulfilment of his quest. It is written on a blackboard by Pomeroy as her parting shot after being sacked, justified by its status as a famous linguist's favourite term in the English language but also an indicator to Donnie of the entrance to Roberta Sparrow's house through which he needs to pass to provoke the attack by Seth that triggers the Ensurance Trap. Donnie utters the phrase during a sequence at the Halloween party in which he seems to pass inside the time travel pathway 'spear' emanating from the body of Gretchen. He repeats it ('huh, cellar door') as he stands outside the door. The connection is made explicitly, at the cellar door, and the attentive viewer might relate it specifically to issues of time travel and destiny, having picked up the significance of its earlier mention inside the spear (additional attention to the phrase is drawn in part of a deleted scene, not included in the director's cut, in Pomeroy's question: 'Will Donnie Darko find his Cellar Door?'). But even with all this

Another hint spelled out to the viewer, in Karen Pomeroy's parting blackboard message

in place – which is far from likely to be the case for all first-time viewers – no explanation other than wild coincidence is provided for the term having first been so clearly drawn to attention by the teacher. That requires understanding of the concept of the Manipulated Living or Dead, from 'The Philosophy of Time Travel'; the suggestion that characters in the Tangent Universe are steering Donnie towards his destiny. This conception is not elaborated at all in the original version, which makes Pomeroy's use of the term puzzling: too precise a connection with subsequent events to be coincidence but lacking any clear, logical explanation. Frank's statement 'They can show you the way', voiced in extra-diegetic space, over one of the inserted titles counting down the days left until the world is due to end, provides a hint. It precedes the scene in which Donnie first raises the subject of time travel with Monnitoff and is given his copy of 'The Philosophy of Time Travel', followed by a discussion of the book and Sparrow's house at the family dinner table. But it is the kind of hint most likely to be picked up retrospectively, only after the viewer has become initiated elsewhere.

The original version of *Donnie Darko* abides by classical convention in some respects more than might initially be apparent. Many events might seem relatively arbitrary or unconnected, for the viewer not equipped with the backstory. They turn out to be tightly linked, however, and highly motivated by the workings of the mechanism through which Donnie is led to his destiny, even if the nature of the mechanism remains unclear. Just about every component of the film can be understood as playing a part in steering him towards the task for which he has been selected (who or what does the selecting is one of the higher-level questions that remains entirely open to speculation in either edition of the film). If the flood causes the school closure that ensures the cementing of a relationship between Donnie and Gretchen, for example, an initial connection is sparked by Pomeroy's announcement that the new girl can sit next to the boy she thinks is the cutest, and by Gretchen's choice of Donnie (the fact that the flood created the possibility of the conversation in which Donnie invites Gretchen to 'go with' him is explicitly acknowledged by the former, a hint to the viewer). Likewise, the burning by Donnie of Jim Cunningham's house reveals the latter's status as a paedophile, thus requiring Farmer to leap to his defence, meaning she cannot accompany Sparkle Motion to Los Angeles. The result is that Rose has to go, leaving Donnie and Elizabeth free to have the Halloween party that sets the climactic events in process (whether it had to be Rose and Samantha on the plane that lost its engine, or had to be that plane, or whether Donnie actually had to die, after somehow putting the engine back into the right time, are all questions that continue to provoke speculation).

Much that might at first appear to be background detail proves to be of more direct salience to the central plot, a further source of reward and currency for those who invest in repeat viewing and/or cult adoption: a red car that passes Donnie on the street in the early scenes can be identified retrospectively as that of Frank, which will play a crucial role later in the springing of the Ensurance Trap; when Donnie tells Gretchen he once accidentally burned down a house, he is walking past Jim Cunningham's, which will suffer a similar fate at his hands; a mysterious figure in a red tracksuit, who appears on two occasions, is one of the Federal Aviation Authority officials investigating the crash of the jet engine; and so on. What turns out to be the very tight plotting of the film is another dimension that becomes most apparent in retrospect, an unusual twist on the classical norm, giving it the quality of what Ed Tan describes as the 'postdictable' (as opposed to the pre-dictable), based on unanticipated turns of events that can be integrated into existing interpretation through a revision of previous assumptions (1996: 134). This is itself motivated to a large extent through the science-fiction/horror/mystery components of the generic mix. It is conventional in the mystery format, for example, for key connections between events to become clear only towards the end. The generic/modality blend offered by *Donnie Darko* complicates this, however, by giving many of the events that turn out to have supernatural explanation what appear to be more quotidian grounding in the emotional lives of the characters (the connections between Donnie, Gretchen and Pomeroy all being potentially attributable to their shared 'outsider' status, for example, as much as any more 'profound' manipulations).

OTHER FORMAL DIMENSIONS

However distinct in some respects, *Donnie Darko* relies on many 'classical' and familiar narrative conventions, not least a basic structure revolving around the actions and dilemmas of a single central protagonist and a relatively small number of other characters, among them helpers and antagonists (and including the near-obligatory romantic subplot, regardless of whether or not it is understood as a function of supernatural intervention). In this respect, it shares with many Hollywood films the use of a basic quest model familiar from a wide range of cultural mythologies and folk tales, although in this case the 'heroic journey' is enacted within what appears on the surface to be the everyday fabric of suburban teenage life.[35] A general reliance on familiar conventions is also found in other formal dimensions such as the manner in which the film is shot and edited. Like most commercially distributed features from Hollywood or the independent sector, *Donnie Darko* relies primarily on formal devices sufficiently familiar to appear largely 'invisible' to the viewer, including standard uses of lenses and shot scales and the conventions of continuity editing. Most of the time these are used in an entirely standard manner. Some departures are found but these are usually subtle, relatively minor and motivated by narrative material; that is to say, departures from convention have a rationale, usually associated with the (actual or potential) supernatural dimensions of the plot.

Examples of both formal convention and motivated departure can be seen in a series of scenes leading up to and including Donnie's first encounter with Frank. The opening sequences are followed by a dinner table scene, a familiar ingredient in the family-drama strand of the film, as suggested above. The dinner table scene is shot in entirely conventional manner, according to the long-standing dictates of continuity editing.[36] An initial long shot of the five family members around the table serves as an establishing shot, making clear the spatial relationships between the characters (Eddie and Rose sitting opposite one another, Donnie on Eddie's right, Samantha and Elizabeth opposite Donnie). A series of eyeline matches maintains and reinforces the impression that the characters continue to inhabit this concrete space (despite the fact that each separate character shot may have been taken separately). As Elizabeth starts a conversation with a provocative opening gambit, aimed chiefly at her father, her eyes shift to her right, towards his direction in the fictional space. Cut to Eddie, his eyes shifting to his left in response. Cut to Rose, her eyes moving in reaction to her right. And so on, throughout the scene, a simple illustration of a basic continuity regime. Each character is framed at the same scale in medium shot, approximately head-and-shoulders/chest (Elizabeth and Samantha, sharing one side of the table, are framed together in a two-shot). For most of the sequence the same framing is used each time we see each character, further maintaining a consistency of scale and position (and also an economic way of shooting the sequence, minimising the need for new camera and lighting set-ups). A slight change of framing is made for some shots of Donnie and Elizabeth/Samantha, however. Towards the latter stages of the conversation, the camera position is rotated a little, catching each slightly more from the side. This coincides with the point at which the dialogue becomes more heated, Donnie and Elizabeth sharing an exchange of expletives ('you're such a fuck-ass'; 'go suck a fuck'). The shift in framing can be read as a subtle way of underlining the shift of mood. Framed a little more side on, each character adopts a slightly more confrontational posture, positioned as looking (or, in Donnie's case, pointing) more overtly towards the other because this now involves a more emphatic look *across* the space of the screen. The fact that the characters inhabit their own spaces throughout the sequence, framed separately (with the exception of Elizabeth and Samantha) might also be read conventionally as emphasising a state of relatively distanced or hostile relationships.

The strategies employed in the construction of this sequence are the basic building blocks of familiar/mainstream cinematic convention, designed to create the impression of the existence of a solid, self-sufficient on-screen fictional universe. They are not meant to be brought to the conscious attention of the viewer, but they can contribute to the creation of specific meanings and interpretations, beyond the initial establishment of dimensions such as the physical space in which the action unfolds. Similarly basic conventional devices are employed in the scene that follows, in which Rose visits Donnie in his bedroom. The scene is constructed through a series of shot/reverse-shots, between Donnie lying on his bed and Rose coming through the door and approaching him in a failed attempt to discover the nature of his night-time movements. Shots of Donnie alternate with shots of Rose, a number of routine devices establishing the spatial and temporal continuity of their exchange (these include further eye-line matches, although Donnie's alienation is signified at first by his specific refusal to look up from the book he is reading when interrupted). The same kind of conventional regime continues across the following scenes in which: Rose exits onto the landing; Rose converses with Eddie in their bedroom (a two-shot here contributing, with the general tone of the exchange, to the creation of an impression that their relationship is reasonably well-grounded); Donnie takes his medication in the bathroom (although viewed only via his reflection in a mirror, sometimes a signifier of the presence of other dimensions); and Eddie wakes later that night and watches the Dukakis/Bush debate on television. The latter ends with the camera moving in for emphasis on the clock as it strikes midnight, the point at which the Tangent Universe is born. This is followed by the first visitation by Frank, a sequence that maintains most of the general 'rules' of continuity/convention but that also offers some more expressive touches that can be interpreted as manifestations of the extra-normal.

After a title caption reading 'October 2 1988' and Frank's 'wake up', an establishing shot is provided: a light going on in an upstairs room, seen from outside. A medium-long shot follows of Donnie sitting up in bed, in a space (his bedroom) already established in the sequence described above. Donnie gets up, apparently in a trance, and walks towards the camera, into a mid-shot and then a closer shot before passing out of frame near to the camera at screen left. As he approaches, the camera tilts upwards to keep him in shot, completing the movement as he leaves the frame, to leave an image tilted up towards the ceiling (partially draped with an American flag). Such a shot is relatively unconventional, although motivated at first by the tilt required to keep the protagonist in shot (a basic convention of character-led narrative). The upward tilt is to some extent answered in the

next shot, in which the camera looks down the main stair-
case of the house ready for Donnie to walk into frame from
the left. Donnie moves into frame again in the next shot, as
he emerges through a doorway into the kitchen and towards
the camera, moving into a close shot of his head as he exits
to screen right with his eyes shut. Next comes a mid-shot of
the front door, seen from the inside, as Frank's voice urges
Donnie to 'come closer'. The camera moves towards the
door, creating the impression that this is Donnie's subjective
point of view (and giving the viewer the sense, along with the
character, of following the injunction to 'come closer'). As the
camera moves forward, it tilts upward, somewhat puzzlingly,
towards a chandelier hanging in the entrance hall. It tilts back
down again, to the door, although now the door is just closing, having previously been already closed. A slight disjunction occurs at this point. If the perspective is Donnie's point
of view, the door might be closing behind who or whatever
he might be following. But this proves not to be the case. The
door does not re-open, as might be expected if Donnie/we
were to follow through it, and the sharp-eyed viewer might
notice a glimpse of colour outside the door, as it closes, that
suggests that Donnie has already passed through, the colour
being the same blue as the shirt he is wearing. Outside, we
are given a long shot of Donnie walking away from the camera down the garden path, the camera rising very slightly.
This is followed by a medium close-up of Donnie's head and
shoulders, centred in the frame and moving slowly towards
the camera. At this point the image dissolves to our first sight
of Frank, standing in long shot on the green at a golf course
to which the scene has shifted. Frank is also centred on the
screen, the dissolve briefly superimposing his image onto
that of Donnie. Frank utters the '28 days...' countdown, after
which another dissolve returns to the previous image of Donnie, over which plays Frank's 'that is when the world will end'

Unmotivated angle: the puzzling upward-tilted shot of the chandelier in the Darko entrance hall, foreshadowing the crash of the jet engine

and Donnie's 'why?', accompanied by a somewhat disturbing smile. After this we are returned via an image of television static to the sequence in the house that culminates in the crash of the jet engine.

Most of this sequence abides by the usual conventions of 'classical' framing and editing, but there are a number of no- ticeable departures. The two upward-tilting shots draw atten- tion to themselves, especially the shot of the chandelier, for which no obvious motivation is apparent and which comes in the middle of a camera movement that offers unusually ambiguous markers of its location (subjective or objective viewpoint). Both upwards shots can easily be understood in retrospect, foreshadowing the crash of the jet engine on the house (through Donnie's ceiling and first registered visually by the shaking of the chandelier), but this is not an interpre- tation available at the time to the uninitiated viewer. It is an- other source of reward for the repeat viewer. The dissolves between the images of Donnie and Frank are also heightened usages, liable to draw the viewer's attention. Although a fa- miliar part of the classical repertoire, the dissolve tends by its nature, superimposing one element on another, to draw attention to the status of its components as constructed/manipulated images. Any such effect is increased in this case by the mirrored framing, a quality potentially recognisable as having been carefully composed and thus *im*posed on (and constructing) the material. The combined effect also seems to invite interpretation – the fact that the image of Frank appears to 'come out of' and return to that of Donnie's head might support any suggestion that the 'Frank' dimension of the film is Donnie's subjective fantasy or hallucination.

The Donnie/Frank sequences include a heightened or more expressive dimension than the immediately preceding domestic scenes, but these effects remain subtle and passing. Most viewers are unlikely to be able to describe the departures illustrated above, or to dwell at all on their potential implications. In general, they are more likely to create an unspecified sense of something being slightly unusual about the sequence. The familiarity of classical strategies is such that they are usually more recognisable in their absence than presence, often by creating a general more than any specific impression of difference from the norm. This is an effect that might seem appropriate to the specific qualities offered by *Donnie Darko*, especially in its original form, as a text characterised by evocations of the otherworldly the precise nature of which are not easy to pin down. However noticeable they might or might not be to the viewer (which depends on the nature and orientation of the individual), any heightening of or departure from classical norms outlined above is motivated by narrative-related content. This clearly situates the film in the broad realm that encompasses both Hollywood and most of the commercially-distributed independent sector, as opposed to parts of the spectrum of what is usually termed art cinema in which formal innovation is in some cases pursued as an end in itself.[37] The same can be said of some more overtly expressive sequences in which the film shifts between normal and manipulated speeds of action.

Blurry fast-motion: time-lapse footage at the entrance to Donnie's school

Fast- and slow-motion effects are used on a number of occasions during *Donnie Darko*, the former in a particularly eye-
catching variety associated primarily with the motions of figures coming and going through the main entrance at Donnie's
school. A camera equipped with an intervelometer device is
used to create a time-lapse effect, in which characters appear
to move very fast because the shutter is fired at discrete in-
tervals. The result is a rapid stuttering kind of movement and
a clear break from what is conventionally taken to be normal
'realistic' cinematography. This kind of fast motion also features in another sequence in which visual stylisation might be

Showy stylisation: the camera turns from its side to an upright position
in the sequence that introduces the school and its principal characters

drawn to the attention of the viewer, the sequence in which we are first introduced to the school and its principal characters. It begins very distinctively, with the camera positioned on its side as Donnie disembarks from the school bus, before righting itself and moving laterally away to the opening piano notes of 'Head Over Heels' by Tears for Fears. A new shot picks up Donnie and two friends inside the door, following them and introducing several other characters in an elaborate unbroken series of steadicam manoeuvres that includes two near-180-degree rapid pans and sped-up sequences involving the movements of Kitty Farmer and Principal Cole (David Moreland). Another eye-catching effect, during the Halloween party sequences towards the end of the film, is a partially sped-up 360-degree rotation of the camera that makes Donnie's figure, framed from the chest up and ending with arms outstretched, appear to cartwheel before the viewer's eyes.

These stylised sequences can be understood on at least two levels. The sequence in the school, especially, can be read as an example of 'showy' cinematography used partly for its own sake, as a source of audio-visual pleasure (orchestration to the song is an important part of the effect) and/or as a way for the director to show off his own ability. It can be seen as an example of self-consciously 'virtuoso' camerawork, part of the function of which, for a first-time feature director, might be to act as a calling card, a demonstration of what he (with the aid of the cinematographer) can achieve. Showiness of this kind is not uncommon in the indie sector, as I have argued elsewhere (King 2005). The same might be said of the intervelometer sequences and the revolving camera. Both effects have potential to contribute to the impression the film offers of departing, if only in relatively small ways, from convention. They are the kind of formal touches that can help to constitute the 'off-beat' impression sought by many independent features. At the same time, however, they can be understood to be motivated by dimensions specific to the material of *Donnie Darko*. The use of fast and slow motion – the latter deployed in the Sparkle Motion performance, intercut with the setting fire of Cunningham's home – entails a manipulation of time that can be taken as a visual correlative of the time travel/alternative universe theme. It creates an impression of extra dimensionality, both generally and in the specific realm of temporal dislocation (an effect underlined by the fact that the school sequence and two of the three intervelometer sequences begin with the slightly distorted tones of a chiming clock). The connection is made more explicitly in the director's cut in Donnie's comment 'we're moving through time' to Gretchen, after a brief passage of intervelometer footage during Cunningham's presentation at the school. In retrospect, or to the viewer of this version, such effects might contribute to a sense of the constructedness and manipulability, the provisional status, of the fabric of a Tangent Universe that can, eventually, be destroyed by the cinematic effect of being fast-rewound. The revolving camera sequence also creates an impression of disjunction, seemingly motivated by Donnie's puzzled expression and the general tendency of this point in the narrative (it might also be taken by horror aficionados as a nod to similarly-motivated camerawork of the same outlandish variety used in *The Evil Dead*).

The use of 'Head Over Heels' in the sequence considered above brings us to another dimension of *Donnie Darko* in which formal qualities are potentially brought to the attention of the viewer. Sound and music generally play an important part in the establishment of mood, tone and modality, as has already been suggested above. Extra-diegetic sound, produced from beyond the confines of the fictional universe, provides a major source of underlying guidance to the viewer, as is conventional across Hollywood and most of the inde-

'Lost in admiration': lyrics that reflect the material on screen, as Principal Cole is introduced to Jim Cunningham

pendent sector. In the case of the songs used in the film, however, the fit between lyrics and the events or characters is on some occasions 'excessively' close, the result of which potentially decreases the extent to which the music might be understood to merge into the general texture of the piece, giving it the status of more overt commentary. 'Head Over Heels' continues in a sequence in the school grounds, for example, including the line 'I'm lost in admiration', voiced at the moment that Principal Cole clutches Jim Cunningham's hand in greeting (Cole will subsequently prove to be excessively enamoured with Cunningham's simplistic morality, as most clearly manifested in the sacking of Pomeroy). Another example comes in the closing lyric 'time flies', sung to the last part of the sequence, in which the intervelometer is used in a rapid-motion time-lapse sequence in Pomeroy's classroom. Song lyrics also add to the infrastructure of more or less exact background plot hints provided by the film, ranging from the 'fate, up against your will' of Echo and the Bunnymen's 'Killing Moon' (applicable to Donnie's situation) and the use of 'Love Will Tear Us Apart' by Joy Division (a diegetic source, the music playing in the fictional background) as Gretchen joins Donnie at the Halloween party shortly before she reaches a Tangent Universe destiny that ensures that the two will never meet in the normal world. Along with some of the other intertexts cited in this chapter, the popular music featured in *Donnie Darko* is part of a structure of references that locates the film in the culture of the late 1980s, an issue to which we now turn in analysis of its social, political and historical contexts.

THE POLITICS OF DARKO: VOTING FOR DUKAKIS?

'I'm voting for Dukakis' are the first words of *Donnie Darko*, uttered by Elizabeth Darko during the dinner table scene outlined above. The line immediately situates the film in a particular historical context, during the Bush/Dukakis presidential election campaign of 1988, a background relevant to a number of issues touched upon by the film. *Donnie Darko* itself is a product of a different historical moment, the late 1990s and early 2000s period during which it was conceived, written, produced and distributed. In this case, however, it is somewhat more difficult to establish an exact or immediate connection with the times, as is often the case. The most obvious link between the film and wider events at the time of release was its resonance with the events of 9/11,

The implicit political message of the film?

as suggested in chapter two. That was a matter purely of co-incidence, however, and of no relevance to an understanding of how the film might be seen as a *product* of its social or historical context. It is relatively rarely the case that films designed for the commercial marketplace can be interpreted as direct responses to immediate events, prevailing social issues or concerns. They tend, instead, to mediate wider social, cultural or political material in a broader and more diffuse manner, as part of the background on which they draw to create an impression of cultural verisimilitude, of unfolding in a fictional world that shares some recognisable characteristics with that of the world beyond the screen. Much of the material explored in *Donnie Darko*, for example, could be said to be of similar relevance to the contexts of both the late 1980s and the period a decade or more later in which the film was created and viewed – particularly the broad questions of 'morality' and 'values' that underpin parts of the narrative background – the former period performing the role of throwing some issues into particularly sharp relief.

The dinner table discussion establishes initial positions in an explicitly political register. Eddie Darko's response to his elder daughter is based on hostility to higher federal government taxes, associated with the Democratic Party candidate. In the politics of the 1980s such issues were overlain to a heightened degree by 'moral' questions, divisions over economic dimensions such as taxation blurring into battles over culture and 'values' along a polarised front between liberal and reactionary forces. Much of the strength of the preceding Ronald Reagan administrations was based on the mobilisation of a fundamentalist religious right-wing constituency that pitched itself against the 'evils' of a liberalism supposed to have held sway since the cultural and political upheavals of the 1960s. A similar division is central to the political axes of *Donnie Darko*. The Christian fundamentalist right is embod-

The two opposing ideological camps at the school

ied by Jim Cunningham and Kitty Farmer, with the allegiance of Principal Cole; the more progressive/liberal opposition by Karen Pomeroy and Kenneth Monnitoff. Pomeroy is sacked, following the controversy stirred up by Farmer in relation to the teaching of 'The Destructors' ('this filth') and it is made clear that Monnitoff's freedom to discuss scientific issues that touch at the boundaries of religious questions is similarly constrained ('I'm not going to be able to continue this con- versation … I could lose my job.'). A direct link between the 'moral' and political dimensions is made in a background dis- cussion between Farmer and a female colleague about their preferred vice-presidential candidate, Dan Quayle (Farmer: 'Nobody cares about responsibility, morality, family values.'). Subliminal references are also made to the ghost of Reagan: a mysterious reflection of his visage in the glass of a book- case in the study of Principal Cole, framed alongside Farmer, and a figure in a Reagan mask at the Halloween party.

The film loads the dice quite heavily against the Cunning- ham/Farmer camp, also seeming to favour Dukakis over Bush (the latter further signified by the choice of subject-matter discussed in the extracts from the campaign debate viewed by Eddie on the night of the jet-engine crash: Dukakis talks about ensuring 'that we never again do business with a

Farmer with Cunningham's simplistic 'Lifeline' axis

drug-running Panamanian dictator, that we never again funnel aide to the Contras from convicted drug dealers'; Bush's response, to an embarrassing chapter in American foreign policy, is rather stumbling and weak). If Cunningham and his 'Lifeline' exercise appears an easy target, Farmer is also a rather crude caricature and frequent source of comic relief. She is made into a silly rather than a threatening character, although she does succeed in getting Pomeroy sacked (in the Tangent Universe, at least), most notably in her demonstration of ignorance about the identity of Graham Greene ('I think we have *all* seen *Bonanza*' [the television series starring Lorne Greene], an arrogantly delivered line designed to make her appear ridiculous). Cunningham is ultimately demonised when it is revealed that he is a paedophile, but his 'motivational' speaking and 'Lifeline' exercise are also depicted as shallow and simplistic. As Donnie points out to Farmer, an attempt to situate all impulses on an axis running between love and fear leaves out 'a whole spectrum of human emotions'. Pomeroy and Monnitoff are much more positively characterised. The party-political and 'morality/values' components are separated out in some instances, however, creating a less reductive impression of the social/political landscape. Eddie and Rose Darko are clearly in favour of Bush over Dukakis, but they appear generally to be liberal parents, in terms of both the freedom they offer their children and their lack of sympathy with the views of Farmer.

Donnie Darko seems to pitch itself clearly against Reagan/Bush era fundamentalism and moral simplicities, a position that might also apply to the politics of its own time, especially given the presence of another Bush in the White House at the time of release. The 'culture wars' of the 1980s had certainly not been resolved by the late 1990s and early 2000s, if anything having been rekindled in the oppositions that characterised the highly-charged and contentious presidential elections that brought George Bush Jr to power in 2000 and kept him there in 2004. The stance of the film in the overtly political arena is hardly surprising for a production aimed at the indie end of the cinematic spectrum, where allegiance with such blatant culturally reactionary forces would be highly unusual. When it comes to the implications of the underlying narrative premises of the film, however, the picture may be somewhat less clear-cut. *Donnie Darko* lends itself quite readily to being understood partly as a Christian allegory, with Donnie as the Christ-like figure who sacrifices himself. This is certainly a reading made, more or less explicitly, by a number of the Amazon reviewers and encouraged, if only in passing, through the film's reference to *The Last Temptation of Christ* (while Cunningham, first glimpsed in an image in which the early sun creates a halo around his head, is condemned by Donnie as 'the fucking Antichrist' and the innocent character of the picked-upon classmate Cherita Chen (Jolene Purdy) performs onstage as the angelic figure she has been taken by some viewers to represent more broadly in the film). It seems justifiable to read some specific significance into the choice of Martin Scorsese's film as a background point of reference, its presence otherwise being thinly motivated as it does not seem a very likely choice to be sharing a Halloween 'Frightmare' double bill with *The Evil Dead*. At the very least, *Donnie Darko* as interpreted by Kelly allows for the existence of a guiding, supernatural force that might be equated with some kind of god. Specifically religious dimensions are raised in the discussions between Donnie and both his therapist and science teacher, although their implications remain ambiguous.

Monnitoff suggests that the appearance of a time travel portal would be 'an act of God'. If God controls time, Donnie replies, all time is pre-decided and follows a set path; and if that path was visible, as experienced by Donnie on some occasions, it would be possible to see into the future. Monnitoff responds that Donnie is contradicting himself: if destiny were visibly manifested, the choice would be available to act differently, putting an end to all preformed destiny. 'Not if you travel in God's channel', says Donnie, but what exactly is meant by this is not made clear. The implication is that he means something like his own ordained destiny, in which case the interpretation of the film falls into a religious domain. This is the point at which Monnitoff says he is unable to continue the conversation for fear of losing his job, an element in establishing the repressive nature of the school regime but also, perhaps, a convenient way for the filmmaker to avoid spelling out the significance of a dimension that might be less appealing to the principal target market for the film. A similar sense of touching on but ultimately skirting questions of religion is found in some of Donnie's exchanges with Thurman. When Donnie confesses to flooding the school and burning down Cunningham's house, he says he has to obey Frank or he will be left alone. 'I won't know his master plan', he adds, to which Thurman asks: 'Do you mean God's master plan? Do you now believe in God?' Donnie does not answer the question. This scene is extended in the director's cut. After informing Donnie that his pills are placebos, Thurman suggests that

Donnie is not an atheist, who denies the existence of God, but an agnostic: 'Someone who believes that there can be no proof of the existence of God but does not deny a possibility that God exists.' This builds on an exchange earlier in the film (in both versions) that follows from Roberta Sparrow's whispered message to Donnie that 'every living creature on earth dies alone'. Thurman asks Donnie if he feels alone. He says he would like to believe not, but does not see any proof and does not debate it any more. It is absurd, he concludes, in response to which Thurman asks: 'The search for God is absurd?' Donnie: 'It is if everyone dies alone.' The career of Sparrow, an important if largely off-screen presence who we are told abandoned a career as a nun to write her book and teach science, suggests a move away from religion and towards the secular realm. *Donnie Darko* itself appears to be agnostic, tending to edge towards and then back away from the potential religious implications of the underlying plot. The result is that the viewer can choose whether or not to understand the film in an explicitly religious context. This is a useful strategy given the potential for an overtly religious dimension to be off-putting to many of those likely to be attracted to the film on the basis of qualities such as its generic and/or more broadly independent or cult status, especially in the light of the negative qualities associated with its representations of Christian fundamentalism.

It is notable that the components of the fear/love opposition around which Cunningham's theology/ideology revolves are mobilised to a significant extent by the film. Donnie might be seen as torn by the rival impulses of his fear of the situation into which he is being drawn and love for those around him (another point of contact with *The Last Temptation of Christ*, the protagonist of which suffers from the same competing feelings). The difference between the film and the world according to Cunningham and Farmer is that in the former the boundaries between such emotions seem far less clear-cut. Human experience is much more complex and multi-dimensional, as Donnie suggests, a complexity not just asserted in dialogue but also embodied in the genre/modality blend from which the film is constituted. Some other connections can be made between these issues and the context in which the film is set. A simplistic message based on the 'fear' component is widely recognised to have been a determining factor in Bush's eventual victory over Dukakis, from an initial position well behind in the polls. The decisive issue in the latter stages of the campaign was the Bush camp's effort to paint Dukakis as soft on crime, principally through the exploitation of an incident involving a convicted murderer, Willie Horton, who committed another assault after escaping during a weekend prison furlough. As one commentator puts it, the campaign said little about many of the issues facing the country at the time 'but it did indicate the extraordinary hold that appeals to law and order, fear, and patriotism still exerted on the American public' (Chafe 1991: 497–8). Attacks on the patriotism of Dukakis focused on the veto he imposed, as governor of Massachusetts, on a law requiring school students to pledge allegiance to the flag. This is an issue unlikely to be picked up by many viewers of *Donnie Darko* in the early 2000s, although two possible points of reference can be found in the film. It seems conspicuous that among Pomeroy's belongings when she leaves the school is her own American flag, an icon the prominence of which might usually be expected to signify more reactionary values than those associated with the character; a flag also appears in Donnie's bedroom, attached to the ceiling through which the jet engine crashes, the significance of which might also be open to debate.

In more general social/cultural terms, *Donnie Darko* invites interpretation as an entry in a long series of representations of contemporary suburban American life, a familiar setting for cinematic and other fictional narratives. The milieu in which most of the events of the film unfold is an affluent, leafy suburbia of large houses and spacious lawns. This is a world in which a certain level of wealth appears to be taken for granted, as does the primarily (although not exclusively) white and middle-class status of those members of the population of Middlesex, and its private, fee-paying school, to whom we are introduced. In this respect, *Donnie Darko* fits a pattern found in many Hollywood and independent films, implicitly propagating a view of suburban America as a place of largely unquestioned material plenty, without any consideration of the issues of class, gender and race on which it might be founded. The film's portrait of suburbia is largely neutral, avoiding either pole of what Robert Beuka describes as a 'restrictive, binary system' in which representations have tended historically either to celebrate suburbia as a harmonious model of community, an achievement of the 'American dream' (an interpretation associated most strongly with 1950s television series such as *Leave it to Beaver* (1957–63)), or to condemn it as a soulless realm of conformity and alienation (2004: 11).

The latter is familiar territory at the satirical end of American cinema, in contemporary independent and studio-distributed features such as *Happiness* (1998) and *American Beauty* (1999). *Donnie Darko* differs from such works in not taking easy pot-shots at aspects of its immediate familial setting (these being reserved for Farmer, Cunningham and Cole). It is significant that the film does not satirise the wife/mother figure, Rose, whose nearest equivalents are subjected to critical treatment in *Happiness* and *American Beauty* as part of a wider cultural tendency to associate some of the ills of suburban life with its allegedly domesticated and emasculating qualities (Beuka 2004: 110, 139). If Donnie is alienated and/or undergoing some kind of teenage rebellion, no specific sources of such an attitude are indicated in the world of his parents, another factor that gives his situation a broader and more nuanced resonance. Rose and Eddie are painted sympathetically, rather than as representatives of negative qualities, as is the maternal presence of Thurman, another 'authority' figure with potential to have been treated less positively (if Rose seems almost always to be accompanied by a glass of wine, this seems to be a response to, rather than the cause of, family tensions). Donnie's problems of adjustment – a history, we are told, that dates back well before the events of the film – might be ascribed to the difficulties faced by an unusually bright, artistic youth brought up in a world of 'soulless' material affluence, but the film provides no particular evidence for such a reading. This dimension of the film might be understood quite generally or in the more specific social/historical context of explorations of teenage angst in the wake of events such as the Columbine High School shootings of 1999,[38] although any such connections are always difficult to pin down in other than very broad terms.

4

PLACING *DONNIE DARKO*

Donnie Darko is in some respects a casebook example of a film that has gained cult status, fulfilling a number of the requirements usually associated with the achievement of such a reputation. It accords with several prevailing definitions of cult film at both the textual and extra-textual levels considered so far in this book, and in the connections between the two. Textual features include its use and mixture of generic elements and the ambiguous nature of central narrative events, especially in the original version. Extra-textual features include the history of the film's release, particularly its initial box-office failure and the manner in which it was subsequently adopted by certain niche audiences. As an example of cult film, it is certainly one that demonstrates the limitations of any definitions of cult that are restricted exclusively to either the textual or the extra-textual, audience-related level. My analysis of *Donnie Darko* accords with Matt Hills' argument that both dimensions of cult should be considered in relation to how they function in specific examples, rather than the category of cult being subject to *a priori* definitions of either kind (Hills

2007). Cult film embodies a fundamental duality, as Hills suggests: even if the category first emerged, historically, as a result of audience responses, it has subsequently developed a momentum that includes its adoption and institutionalisation, variously, by filmmakers, the film industry and commentators ranging from the journalistic to the academic, to a point at which no component in the process of cult formation can be given universal privilege. If *Donnie Darko* fits the bill in many of these respects, there remain some dimensions in which its particular claim to cult status might be challenged, or at least qualified, although this is a potentially contentious business given the range of investments that have existed in one or another particular definition of the term.

Compared with some examples, often described as cult 'classics', *Donnie Darko* might be described as a rather 'light-weight' variety of cult film, on more than one count. At the textual level, *Donnie Darko* fits only to a limited extent with an understanding of cult film as often involving *transgressions* of cinematic or cultural norms and conventions, a key aspect of the text-based definition of cult suggested by J. T. Telotte and Barry Keith Grant among other academic commentators (Telotte 1991a; Grant 1991 and 2000). The principal form of transgression found in *Donnie Darko* is its blurring of genre boundaries, a feature also of some entries in the repertoire of more established cult classics, most notably *The Rocky Horror Picture Show*, with its mixture of elements of horror, science fiction and the musical. But *Donnie Darko* is not a transgressive text in the wider or more radical senses in which the term is often used. It is not a film that set out to be, or has achieved a reputation for being, provocative or 'shocking' as a way of marking out difference from the commercial mainstream. It does not push at the boundaries of what would generally be seen as more broadly acceptable, in terms of either the 'morality' or otherwise of represented character behaviour or more specifically cinematic dimensions such as the limits imposed by censorship or classification. It differs in these respects from the transgressions celebrated in canonical cult features such as *The Texas Chain Saw Massacre* (1974) and *Pink Flamingos*. *Donnie Darko* is not characterised by the 'excess' associated with such films, and the midnight movie variety of cult film more generally (see, for example, Studlar 1991; Hoberman & Rosenbaum 1991). It is a far more restrained product, both formally, as suggested in the previous chapter, and at the level of its fictional events.

In comparison with the other titles cited above, *Donnie Darko* seems a very safe and unthreatening form of cult cinema. Any questioning of the film's cult credentials on this level can also be related to the relative ease with which it achieved such status. *Donnie Darko* was not a film that had to languish for a long period in obscure corners of subculture, even if it was relegated for some months to the midnight movie circuit. It received prominent mainstream reviews on initial release, some of them positive and approving, and remains very much a part of the commercially-oriented indie sector rather than its more marginal realms. It has not been rescued from any long-term obscurity or required a passage of many years before gaining cult recognition. Instead, it is the kind of film to which the seemingly oxymoronic label 'instant cult classic' is sometimes attached. Can there be such a thing as an 'instant' cult classic, given the usual requirement for both 'cult' and 'classic' status to require proving over more substantial periods of time? A useful way to begin to answer this question is to use the distinction suggested by Bruce Kawin between 'inadvertent' and 'programmatic' varieties of cult film (1991). The former, of which Kawin's initial example is *Casablanca* (1942), applies to films that have gained cult status for reasons that might never have been anticipated from their original qualities or status. The programmatic cult film is one that has been consciously designed with cult status in mind. Kawin's main examples of the latter are both sequels, *Evil Dead II* (1987) and *The Texas Chain Saw Massacre 2* (1986), each of which can be assumed to have been made deliberately to build on the cult reputation already acquired by its predecessor.

Given these two alternatives, *Donnie Darko* might be thought to lie closer to the second category, the programmatic, although a good deal of middle ground seems to exist between the polarities suggested by Kawin. The makers/distributors of the original *Evil Dead* and *The Texas Chain Saw Massacre* might have had reason to expect their films to gain something like cult status, even if less blatantly than their sequels, on the basis of their intrinsic generic and other textual qualities. A more nuanced definition of cult can result from an initial separation of the textual and extra-textual dimensions. *The Evil Dead* and *The Texas Chain Saw Massacre* may not fit Kawin's bill as entirely programmatic cult features, as they could not be so readily assured in advance of their audience take-up and the particular status each would gain in and after its own time. But each is designed in such a way as to lend itself to the likelihood of cult or similar adoption by particular audiences, in a manner that is distinct from the entirely inadvertent cult status gained by an example such as *Casablanca*. This is increasingly the case with the historical establishment of 'cult' as a commercial institution, even if relatively marginal, in the post-war decades (Jancovich 2002). Much the same might be said of *Donnie Darko*, and perhaps more so. It is a film that signals quite explicitly its ready availability for cultish adoption, a fact that – assuming that this is judged to have been done effectively – helps to explain the attribution of the 'instant cult' label. It joins earlier films such as *Liquid Sky* (1982), *Repo Man* (1984) and *Blue Velvet* (1986) as an example of what Grant terms 'the fast food of cult', as

Pitching for cult status?: The bill for the midnight screening attended by Donnie and Gretchen

opposed to 'slowly simmered' texts that take longer to gain such status (1991: 123). Overt markers of this more calculated prospective cult positioning include some of the intertexts considered in the previous chapter, most notably the presence of *The Evil Dead* and the midnight screening context in which it is attended by Donnie and Gretchen. The deliberate decision to leave the original version highly ambiguous can also be seen as a pitch for potential cult status. Once established, the cult reputation of the original was explicitly traded upon in the release of the director's cut, as seen in the trailer examined in chapter three and one of the features included on the director's cut DVD, 'They Made Me Do It Too: The Cult of *Donnie Darko*', which focuses on the establishment of its reputation in the UK.

The cult standing of the film might seem to be part of a cynical niche-marketing strategy as much as genuine adoption by viewers, but there is a general consensus among theorists that cult status cannot simply be manufactured. It is difficult to design a film for cult status, suggests Telotte, 'since many films that gain a cult label and following are never successful through normal patterns of distribution. In fact, many seem to become cult works largely because their audience – their potential lovers – *cannot* be accurately assessed through conventional wisdom, much less segmented and targeted' (1991a: 8). It was clearly not the intention of the filmmaker or distributor that *Donnie Darko* should fail at the box office and rely on a cult reputation established initially through midnight movie screenings and extra-textual material. Broader initial success would clearly have been preferable, although the achievement of cult status has a particular commercial appeal of its own, based on the long-term nature of the revenues that can be achieved by films that remain longer than usual in circulation (Kawin 1991: 22). It remains the case, however, that the film has particular textual characteristics that might have been designed, explicitly or otherwise, to create the potential for cult appeal, regardless of the exact nature of its eventual performance in the marketplace. These include its generally 'dark' nature, often associated with cult, a primary youthful or young-adult target market, as suggested in the previous chapter, and the considerable scope the film offers for the establishment of stronger than usual emotional and cognitive relationships between viewer and text. The emotional dimension, as Kawin suggests, is an important part of the attachment required if films are to be adopted as objects of cult veneration; a sense of ownership and/or validation on the part of the viewer:

> In the case of oldies like *Casablanca*, it is because we have enjoyed and allowed ourselves to feel open to them for so long; in the case of oddities like *Eraserhead* or *Liquid Sky*, it is perhaps because we made them hits, or perhaps because we found there the mirrors for which we were searching, the mirrorings of our buried concerns, our true self-images, and the outrageous projections of nightmare, of rebellion, or of style: a vision that, if not literally ours, still clicked with or spoke to ours. (1991: 20)

In the case of *Donnie Darko*, it is more likely to be the latter effect, rooted for a youth/young-adult audience perhaps in the broader relationship of the film's events with more everyday coming-of-age difficulties, as suggested in the previous chapter, but given greater-than-usual potency through the ambiguous manner in which quotidian and more fantastic dimensions are blurred. A sense of extended viewer relationship with the text might also result from the cognitive engagement required if the ending and broader implications of the film are to be understood and/or subject to the kind of speculation and discussion that continues to characterise online forums.

Donnie Darko does reach out towards the broader mainstream, however, as well as offering these more particular sources of appeal/adoption, a respect in which it differs from the midnight movies considered by Bruce Kawin or J. Hoberman and Jonathan Rosenbaum. It might be understood as a hybrid product, a dimension in which it is not alone among its contemporaries. Attention to cult films has tended to focus disproportionately at the more transgressive or excessive end of the spectrum, partly because such works lend themselves more easily to the applications of certain kinds of theories prevailing in particular academic/theoretical conjunctures (especially the celebration of 'transgression') and partly because of the preferences (cinematic and theoretical) of the most prominent writers on the subject. As Mark Jancovich, Antonio Lázarro Reboll, Julian Stringer and Andy Willis suggest, 'the "cult movie" is an essentially eclectic category', although this comes in a collection of essays the subtitle of which suggests its own particular slant, 'the cultural politics of oppositional taste' (2003: 1). *Donnie Darko* cannot really be understood as an 'oppositional' text, in any substantial manner, but the same can be said of other cult films. As both Telotte and Grant suggest, the transgressive, challenging or oppositional dimension of cult films, even the more extreme varieties, are generally contained by counter-dynamics (in Grant's account, this is often achieved through a caricature treatment of the transgressive 'Other' that makes it less potentially threatening to the viewer). Cult films, including *Donnie Darko*, characteristically offer markers of difference and distinction from what is understood to constitute the mainstream, but these are blended, in variable combination, with more familiar dynamics.[39]

The appeal of such texts can be understood in the context of the wider landscape of cultural consumption, as suggested briefly in the introduction and in relation to some of the Amazon reviews considered in chapter three. Patterns of cultural consumption are closely connected with processes through which distinctions are made between and within different social classes, generations or groups defined on other grounds. Viewers who invest in cult films can be understood, in this way, as marking themselves off from others on the basis of their choice of more or less exclusive or niche products, distinguished to varying extents from those constructed as belonging to the mainstream. The choice of cultural products implies a distinct social-cultural stance or position on the part of the viewer (although these can be complex, especially given the likelihood that many viewers will consume across a range of different kinds of products). A key dimension of this process is the expenditure of what Pierre Bourdieu (1984) terms 'cultural capital', the learned resources and disposition required for the ability to access and take pleasure from more specialised realms of cultural production, particularly those recognised and validated by the 'official' arbiters of culture. Cultural capital is strongly related to class location, being acquired through a combination of inheritance, family upbringing and formal education. More directly applicable to the specific pleasure of cult films is Sarah Thornton's (1995) notion of 'subcultural' capital: knowledge and understanding of cultural products the cachet of which lies in its sense of existing in opposition to the values of the mainstream.

If the pleasurable consumption of films located as works of art cinema requires the mobilisation of officially-recognised cultural capital, the full enjoyment of many cult films requires investment in its subcultural equivalent. The distinction may be far from absolute, however, as seems to be the case with *Donnie Darko*. To enjoy the particular qualities of the film to the full might entail the deployment of elements of each kind of capital. Narrative obliqueness or ambiguity is the familiar material of art or indie cinema, requiring an investment of particular cognitive skills or effort that would be recognised as valuable by the guardians of official and/or academic culture. Familiarity with the film's intertexts would range more widely across the cultural spectrum, however, from the relatively higher/literary culture of Graham Greene to the middle-brow Richard Adams and the 'lower' cultural realms of Stephen King novels, *The Evil Dead* and the 1980s youth movies of John Hughes. The general tendency is towards darker aspects of the popular/'lower' culture end of the spectrum, including numerous dimensions in which the film provides scope for the mobilisation of particular aspects of subcultural capital that might be in the possession of the viewer (the knowledge, for example, that the place of *The Evil Dead* was originally to have been taken by *C.H.U.D.* (1984), as revealed by Kelly in the original director's commentary; or, beyond that, familiarity with *C.H.U.D.* itself, a lesser-known film than *The Evil Dead*, and therefore richer in potential for the exercise of subcultural capital; Donnie also makes a muttered reference to the film – 'he's a fucking C.H.U.D.' – when railing against Cunningham to Gretchen, a comment that is both difficult to pick up and only likely to have meaning to a particular constituency of viewers).

Donnie Darko is not an exclusive text, however. Specific subcultural background, resources or investments such as knowledge of intertexts – or even of the website pages from 'The Philosophy of Time Travel' in relation to the original version – are not *required* for its enjoyment, a key aspect of its location towards the more mainstream and accessible end of the cult spectrum. Some of these competencies might be expected of those who wish to take their involvement further. Moderators of forums such as the Pro Boards fan-site tend to refer new members/posters to extra-textual sources such as the official *Donnie Darko* website or DVD commentaries, suggesting that these be checked first before questions are asked to which they might already hold the answers, but this is not essential for engagement at this level.

Donnie Darko provides scope for different degrees of engagement, the mobilisation of more specialised forms of subcultural capital being available as an optional extra for those sufficiently inclined, a quality it shares with some other relatively mainstream examples including *Kill Bill: Vol. 1* (2003) and *Kill Bill: Vol. 2* (2004).[40] The concept of the 'mainstream', against or in relation to which cult films are often defined, is itself a construct, however, often asserted rhetorically as a negative point of reference that obscures many shades of difference on all sides (Thornton 1995, Jancovich 2002). The mainstream, in its dominant usage, is not simply a negative 'other' to *Donnie Darko*, but one of its constituent ingredients, as has been argued in this book. Like many features that have gained cult status, *Donnie Darko* draws on a mixture of qualities, the precise combination of which account for its particular location in the wider cinematic spectrum. In the rival pulls it manifests between 'mainstream' and more obviously or potentially 'cult' dimensions, it offers useful illustration of the complex manner in which the two are often intertwined. This is further complicated, in the case of *Donnie*

Darko, by the fact that its location has shifted during the life-cycle of the film, especially in its move from the ambiguity of the original to the more narratively-explicit director's cut. The irony is that the release of the director's cut might be interpreted as a final mark of recognition of the film's cult status, a status that might have been reduced (although a good deal of potential for cult adoption would still have existed) had it been released in that form from the start.

At the level of narrative comprehension the elaboration provided by the director's cut (situated at the heart of the diegesis) might seem to move *Donnie Darko* more to the mainstream than the cult end of the spectrum. The release of a second edition of this kind was also the culmination of a process that sought to draw on and extend other dimensions of the film's cult appeal, however, particularly in the offering of additional extras most likely to be appreciated by aficionados. If there appears to be a contradiction here, in the relative pulls between some aspects of greater or lesser basis for cult appeal, it can be understood as a further manifestation of the multiple dimensions in which cult status exists. In the case of *Donnie Darko*, textual and extra-textual elements appear to interact in a manner that is sometimes mutually reinforcing but also sometimes more contradictory (in addition to the fact that what began as one key extra- or para-textual element, the explanation provided in the pages of 'The Philosophy of Time Travel', became a key part of the textual in the director's cut). The broader point this illustrates is that different dimensions of cult status can coexist or develop in an autonomous or semi-autonomous manner. The question of different degrees and kinds of cult status – which seems central to our understanding of how *Donnie Darko* is placed in the film spectrum or the wider cultural landscape – is not simple or one-dimensional, but one that can involve complex processes of negotiation and change.

NOTES

1   I am using 'independent' here to refer to the particular form that
    came to prominence in the late 1980s and 1990s, often referred to
    as 'indie' to distinguish it from a more literal use of the term that
    embraces a broader cinematic spectrum.

2   This was particularly the case for British releases, trading on the
    greater theatrical success of *Donnie Darko* in the UK market, as
    detailed in the following chapter.

3   For the most detailed account of this and other aspects of the pro-
    duction process, see the interview with Richard Kelly in Kevin Con-
    roy Scott (2003); I have also drawn on interviews in the trade press
    cited separately.

4   This and the following detail comes from the '*Donnie Darko* Pro-
    duction Diary' on the director's cut DVD and Poster's commentary.

5   The term is used in Mohr (2001a, 2001b).

6   Box-office figures for *Memento* are from the Internet Movie Data-
    base (imdb.com).

7   These, along with the theatrical trailer, are in the 'special features'
    section of the DVD.

8   Box-office and screen figures are from the 'box office and busi-
    ness' entry for the film in the Internet Movie Database (imdb.com),
    although the figures are also widely cited elsewhere. There is some
    dispute as to whether the film opened in eight or ten markets; I
    have relied on the figure given by Kelly in Scott (2003: xlix).

9   Kelly's view on this issue is also cited by Scott Tobias (2003).

10 Overtly interpretive activity of this kind can be distinguished in a case such as *Donnie Darko* from the ongoing cognitive processing of information entailed in narrative comprehension more generally; on the latter, see Edward Branigan (1992).

11 Soap opera can gain cult status of its own kind, however, although this is likely to rest on grounds other than those of unresolved narrative.

12 For one lengthy series of interpretations and questions, see gnovies .com/discussion/donnie+darko.html.

13 See 'They Made Me Do It Too: The Cult of *Donnie Darko*' featurette on the director's cut DVD and Scott 2003: xlv–xlvi.

14 See, respectively, reviews by Christopher Tookey (2002); Peter Bradshaw (2002); Philip French (2002); Sukhdev Sandhu (2002); Neil Roberts (2002).

15 See, for example, John Robinson (2004).

16 To access on region 2 original, highlight 'special features' on main menu and press 'right' arrow on DVD remote control.

17 Not all press devoted separate reviews to the director's cut. None are listed in the online archives of *The New York Times* or the *New York Post*, two of the sources sampled in the previous chapter, although both provided news/feature articles on the re-release.

18 A total of 927 reviews accessed on 6 March 2006, from which I have taken a sample of 900. The same list of reviews is linked to entries for both the original version and the director's cut. This is a self-selected sample, although substantial, and should not, therefore, be seen as representative of all viewers in any strict sense. An additional 109 web reviews were consulted at www.geocities.com/dark-omovie.reviews.html, May 2006, and other web postings at various times in 2006 including those on the 'message boards' of the Internet Movie Database, starting at http://us.imdb.com/title/tt0246578/board?p=1, and relevant Yahoo groups, starting at http://groups.yahoo.com/search?query=donnie%2Bdarko&submit=Search.

19 64 respondents express an opinion (of approximately 300 reviews posted after the release of the director's cut): 38 favour the original, 17 the director's cut, with nine undecided or seeing merits in each. These are relatively small numbers, given the overall size of the sample, but reviews posted on amazon.com vary considerably in their substance and points of focus.

20 In attributing quotations I have used the details in the form provided

by the reviewer rather than seeking to impose any consistent format.

21 A similar emphasis is found in many of the reviews at geocities. com cited in note 18 above, and more widely in positive internet postings.

22 A weighting towards positive reviews is generally to be expected in such samples, in which enthusiasts are probably more likely to make the effort to post feedback.

23 Five screen pages worth of questions accessed between March 2006 and May 2007 begin at http://darkomovie.proboards24.com/index.cgi?board=ending&page=1.

24 Starting at http://us.imdb.com/title/tt0246578/board?p=1.

25 On psychological realism in texts the events of which might seem unlikely, see Ien Ang's study of the television series *Dallas* (1989: 47). Differences of modality can also be found within genres such as horror, some examples of which use signifiers such as hand-held camerawork or a contemporary setting to create a stronger impression of reality within the generic framework.

26 For Matt Hills (2005) this is an important dimension of many horror films, its significance increased in this case by the relatively small specifically 'horror' component of *Donnie Darko*.

27 Another example in which horror/generic and teen-reality dimensions are kept in relatively close proximity is *Ginger Snaps* (2000), in which werewolf transformations are situated in the context of the onset of female menstruation. This example is also interesting as one in which audience studies showed that some who liked the film did so on this basis, as a way of distinguishing it from an understanding of 'horror films' more generally; see Martin Barker *et al.* (2006). A notable example from television is the long-running *Buffy the Vampire Slayer* (1997–2003), where implication effects are generated by long-term character development and another blurring of horror and more quotidian teen-development dilemmas, although with abrupt transitions into some more formulaic action-horror routines.

28 Giles Edwards, Metrodome, personal communication, May 2007.

29 Further parallels are suggested on the fan-site 'cellar door', from which I have taken the link made specifically between golf course and rabbit hole, including the process of shrinking and growing tall undergone by Alice and the superhuman strength gained by Donnie; see http://www.ruinedeye.com/cd/symbol/htm, accessed

March 2006.

30   For more detail, see the 'cellar door' site, as mentioned above.

31   For more on the particular pleasure offered by the late twist/shock-revelation variety, see Hills 2005: 40–4.

32   Another, more oblique, King reference is the book being read in bed by Eddie, a hardback copy of *The Tommyknockers* (1987), the dust-jacket of which Kelly says in the commentary had been stolen by a member of the crew, leaving the book hard to identify on screen.

33   Another textural reference used by Kelly, cited in the same interview, was Jordan Cronenweth's cinematography in *Peggy Sue Got Married* (1986), another time travel narrative.

34   In addition to art and independent films, such 'puzzle film' qualities have also characterised some Hollywood products and works that straddle the independent/Hollywood divide, as suggested by David Bordwell (2006). The notion that repeated viewing brings pleasure through the revelation of previously unnoticed features is also expressed by multiple viewers of more conventional Hollywood films, however (Klinger 2006: 159).

35   For the classic study of the hero's journey as a narrative archetype, see Joseph Campbell (1949). For an application of Campbell to film narrative, see Christopher Vogler (1992).

36   For an outline of the conventions of continuity editing, see David Bordwell and Kristen Thompson (1997: 284–9).

37   For the classic statement of this division, in the relationship between narrative and form, see Bordwell (1986). Even in the realm of art cinema as defined by Bordwell, however, formal innovation is usually motivated: subjectively, by claims towards verisimilitude, or as a marker of authorial expressivity.

38   Another example that might be cited in the same general context is Sofia Coppola's darkly comic and similarly enigmatic *The Virgin Suicides* (1999).

39   As well as being targeted at a youth/young-adult audience, cult films are also associated primarily with middle-class viewers, according to Mark Jancovich *et al.* (2003) and J. P. Telotte (1991a); cult films, and the understandings through which they are distinguished from the mainstream, also tend to be gendered, privileging the masculine, as argued by Joanne Hollows (2003) and Jacinda Read (2003).

40   For a detailed analysis of this aspect of the *Kill Bill* films, see Geoff King (2008).

BIBLIOGRAPHY

Addiego, W. (2004) 'Teen, sinister rabbit get second chance', *San Francisco Chronicle* (4 September), http://www.sfgate.com/cgi-bin/article.cgi?f=/c/a/2004/09/04/DDGB18I3VE1.DTL&hw=donnie+darko&sn=002&sc=889 (accessed January 2007).

Ang, I. (1989) *Watching Dallas: Soap Opera and the Melodramatic Imagination.* London: Routledge.

Axmaker, S. (2004) 'Added footage gives "Darko" new depth', *Seattle Post-Intelligencer* (2 June), http://seattlepi.nwsource.com/movies/175892_donnie02q.html (accessed January 2007).

Barker, M., E. Mathijs and X. Mendik (2006) 'Menstrual Monsters: The Reception of the *Ginger Snaps* Cult Horror Franchise', *Film International*, 4, 2, 68–77.

Beuka, R. (2004) *SuburbiaNation: Reading Suburban Landscape in Twentieth-Century American Fiction and Film.* New York: Palgrave Macmillan.

Bordwell, D. (1986) *Narration in the Fiction Film.* London: Routledge.

____ (2006) *The Way Hollywood Tells It: Story and Style in Modern Movies.* Berkeley: University of California Press.

Bordwell, D. and K. Thompson (1997) *Film Art: An Introduction*, fifth edition. New York: McGraw-Hill.

Bourdieu, P. (1984) *Distinction: A Social Critique of the Judgement of Taste.* London: Routledge.

Bradshaw, P. (2002) '*Donnie Darko*', *Guardian* (25 October), http://film.guardian.co.uk/News_Story/Critic_Review/Guardian_Film_of_the_

week/0,,818425,00.html (accessed January 2007).

_____ (2004) 'Donnie Darko: The Director's Cut', Guardian (27 August), http://film.guardian.co.uk/News_Story/Critic_Review/Guardian_ review/0,,1291437,00.html (accessed January 2007).

Branigan, E. (1992) Narrative Comprehension and Film. London: Routledge.

Burnett, A. (2004) '"Donnie Darko: The Director's Cut": The Strange Afterlife of an Indie Cult Film', indieWIRE (22 July), http://www.indiewire.com/movies/movies_040722darko.html (accessed January 2007).

Campbell, J. (1949) The Hero with a Thousand Faces. Princeton: Princeton University Press.

Chafe, W. (1991) The Unfinished Journey: America Since World War II, second edition. New York and Oxford: Oxford University Press.

Chagollan, S. (2001) 'Sundance produces a new crop of auteurs', Variety (9 March), http://www.variety.com/article/VR1117795024.html? categoryid=2397&cs=1 (accessed January 2007).

Ebert, R. (2001) 'Donnie Darko', Chicago Sun-Times (26 October), http://rogerebert.suntimes.com/apps/pbcs.dll/article?AID=/20011026/REVIEWS/110260302/1023 (accessed January 2007).

_____ (2004) 'Donnie Darko: The Director's Cut', Chicago Sun-Times (20 August), http://rogerebert.suntimes.com/apps/pbcs.dll/article?AID=/20040820/REVIEWS/408200303/1023 (accessed January 2007).

Fiske, J. (1992) 'The Cultural Economy of Fandom', in Lisa Lewis (ed.) The Adoring Audience: Fan Culture and Popular Media. London: Routledge, 30–49.

French, P. (2002) 'Into the heart of Darko', Observer (27 October), http://film.guardian.co.uk/News_Story/Critic_Review/Observer_Film_of_ the_week/0,,820029,00.html (accessed January 2007).

Graham, B. (2001) 'Donnie Darko', San Francisco Chronicle (26 October), http://www.sfgate.com/cgi-bin/article.cgi?f=/c/a/2001/10/26/DD32 009.DTL&hw=donnie+darko&sn=001&sc=1000 (accessed January 2007).

Grant, B. K. (1991) 'Science Fiction Double Feature: Ideology in the Cult Film', in J. P. Telotte (ed.) The Cult Film Experience: Beyond All Reason. Austin: University of Texas Press, 122–37.

_____ (2000) 'Second Thoughts on Double Features: Revisiting the Cult Film', in X. Mendik and G. Harper (eds) Unruly Pleasures: The Cult Film and its Critics. Guildford: FAB Press, 15–27.

Hills, M. (2002) *Fan Cultures*. London and New York: Routledge.

___ (2005) *The Pleasures of Horror*. London: Continuum.

___ (2007) 'The Question of Genre in Cult Film and Fandom: Between Contract and Discourse', in J. Donald and M. Renov (eds) *The Sage Handbook of Film Studies*. London: Sage.

Hoberman, J. (2001) 'Meet the Depressed', *Village Voice* (24–30 October), http://www.villagevoice.com/film/0143,hoberman,29335,20. html (accessed January 2007).

Hoberman, J. and J. Rosenbaum (1991) *Midnight Movies*. New York: Da Capo Press.

Hodge, R. and D. Tripp (1986) *Children and Television: A Semiotic Approach*. Cambridge: Polity Press.

Hollows, J. (2003) 'The Masculinity of Cult', in M. Jancovich, L. Reboll, J. Stringer and A. Willis (eds) *Defining Cult Movies: The Cultural Politics of Oppositional Taste*. Manchester: Manchester University Press, 35–53.

Hundley, J. (2001) 'Interview: The Outsider; Richard Kelly Breaks In with "*Donnie Darko*"', *indieWIRE* (24 October), http://www.indiewire.com/people/int_Kelly_Richard_011024.html (accessed January 2007).

Jancovich, M. (2002) 'Cult Fictions: Cult Movies, Subcultural Capital and the Production of Cultural Distinctions', *Cultural Studies*, 16, 2, 306–22.

Jancovich, M., L. Reboll, J. Stringer and A. Willis (2003) (eds) *Defining Cult Movies: The Cultural Politics of Oppositional Taste*. Manchester: Manchester University Press.

Kawin, B. (1991) 'After Midnight', in J. P. Telotte (ed.) *The Cult Film Experience: Beyond All Reason*. Austin: University of Texas Press, 18–25.

Kelly, R. (2003) '*Donnie Darko* screenplay', in K. C. Scott *The Donnie Darko Book*. London: Faber, 1–105.

King, G. (2005) *American Independent Cinema*. London: I. B. Tauris.

___ (2008) *Indiewood, USA: Where Hollywood meets Independent Cinema*. London: I. B. Tauris.

Klinger, B. (2006) *Beyond the Multiplex: Cinema, New Technologies, and the Home*. Berkeley: University of California Press.

Lim, D. (2004) 'Tracking Shots', *Village Voice* (20 July), http://www.village voice.com/film/0429,lim2,55218,20.html (accessed January 2007).

Lumenick, L. (2001) 'A "Darko" Victory', *New York Post* (26 October), http://nypost.com/cgi-bin/printfriendly.pl (accessed January 2007).

Mitchell, E. (2001) 'He Has a 6-Foot Rabbit. Does That Mean He's Crazy?', *New York Times* (26 October 2001), http://movies2.nytimes.com/mem/movies/review.html?_r=2&res=9C07E1DB1331F935A15 753C1A9679C8B63&oref=slogin (accessed January 2007).

Mohr, I. (2001a) 'Buying tide out at Sundance', *Hollywood Reporter* (22 January), http://www.hollywoodreporter.com/hr/search/article_display.jsp?vnu_content_id=662250 (accessed January 2007).

____ (2001b) 'Festival sales sky cloudy', *The Hollywood Reporter* (29 January), http://www.hollywoodreporter.com/hr/search/article_display.jsp?vnu_content_id=821759 (accessed January 2007).

Nechak, P. (2001) '"*Donnie Darko*" is a compelling commentary on misfit youths', *Seattle Post-Intelligencer* (26 October), http://seattlepi.nwsource.com/movies/44165_donniedarko26q.shtml (accessed January 2007).

Purdie, S. (1993) *Comedy: The Mastery of Discourse*. New York: Harvester Wheatsheaf.

Read, J. (2003) 'The Cult of Masculinity: From Fan-boys to Academic Bad-boys', in M. Jancovich, L. Reboll, J. Stringer and A. Willis (eds) *Defining Cult Movies: The Cultural Politics of Oppositional Taste* Manchester: Manchester University Press, 54–70.

Roberts, N. (2002) '*Donnie Darko*; At the movies; Film', *The Sun* (26 October), http://thesun.newsint-archive.co.uk/support/dp.asp?doc=TSN-20021026-E-933806 (accessed January 2007).

Robinson, J. (2004) 'Pieces of eighties', *Guardian* (24 April), http://arts.guardian.co.uk/features/story/0,,1200902,00.html (accessed January 2007).

Roxborough, S. (2003) 'U.K. DVD sales of "*Donnie Darko*" help TV Loonland', *Hollywood Reporter* (2 September), http://www.hollywoodreporter.com/hr/search/article_display.jsp?vnu_content_id=821759 (accessed January 2007).

Sandhu, S. (2002) 'Skewed, scary, very beguiling', *Daily Telegraph*, (25 October), http://www.telegraph.co.uk/arts/main.jhtml?xml=/arts/2002/10/25/bfdarko25.xml (accessed September 2007).

____ (2004) '*Donnie Darko*: director's cut', *Daily Telegraph* (27 August), http://www.telegraph.co.uk/arts/main.jhtml?xml=/arts/2004/08/27/bfss27.xml (accessed January 2007).

Scott, K. C. (2003) 'Asking Cosmic Questions: Interview with Richard Kelly', in K. C. Scott *The Donnie Darko Book*. London: Faber, ix–lii.

Shary, T. (2002) *Generation Multiplex: The Image of Youth in Contem-*

porary American Cinema. Austin: University of Texas Press.

Snyder, G. (2004) 'Newmarket turning on light for "Darko"', *Variety* (20 April), http://www.variety.com/article/VR1117903562.html?category id=1236&cs=1&query=snyder+darko (accessed January 2007).

Stuart, J. (2001) 'Movie Review: "*Donnie Darko*"', *Los Angeles Times* (26 October), http://www.calendarlive.com/movies/reviews/cl-movie 000085144oct26,0,5590055. Story (accessed January 2007).

Studlar, G. (1991) 'Midnight S/Excess: Cult Configurations of "Femininity" and the Perverse', in J. P. Telotte (ed.) *The Cult Film Experience: Beyond All Reason.* Austin: University of Texas Press, 138–55.

Tan, E. (1996) *Emotion and the Structure of Narrative Film.* Mahwah, NJ: Erlhaum.

Telotte, J. P. (1991a) 'Beyond all Reason: The Nature of the Cult', in J. P. Telotte (ed.) *The Cult Film Experience: Beyond All Reason.* Austin: University of Texas Press, 5–17.

____ (1991b) 'The Midnight Movie', in J. P. Telotte (ed.) *The Cult Film Experience: Beyond All Reason.* Austin: University of Texas Press, 103–5.

Thomas, K. (2004) '*Donnie Darko*: The Director's Cut', *Los Angeles Times* (23 July), http://www.calendarlive.com/movies/reviews/cl-et-donnie23jul23,2,6147896.story (accessed January 2007).

Thornton, S. (1995) *Club Cultures: Music, Media and Subcultural Capital.* Cambridge: Polity Press.

Tobias, S. (2003) 'Gifted Class', *Hollywood Reporter* (5 August), http://www.hollywoodreporter.com/hr/search/article_display.jsp?vnu-content_id=1000460118 (accessed January 2007).

Todorov, T. (1975) *The Fantastic: A Structural Approach to a Literary Genre.* Ithaca: Cornell University Press.

Tookey, C. (2002) '*Donnie Darko*', *Daily Mail* (25 October), http://www.dailymail.co.uk/pages/live/articles/showbiz/showbiznews.html?in_article_id=144563&in_page_id=1773 (accessed January 2007).

Tulloch, J. and M. Alvarado (1983) *'Doctor Who': The Unfolding Text.* London: Macmillan.

Vogler, C. (1992) *The Writer's Journey: Mythic Structure for Writers.* Studio City: Michael Wiese Productions.

Williams, D. E. (2001) 'Trend: Indies going H'wood', *Hollywood Reporter* (24 January), http://www.hollywoodreporter.com/hr/search/article_display.jsp?vnu_content_id=663931 (accessed January 2007).

INDEX